A BACKWOODSMAN'S YEAR

A
Backwoodsman's
Year

R. W. F. POOLE

Illustrations by Reginald Bass

LARGE PRINT

Oxford, England
Santa Barbara, California

Published in Large Print 1990 by Clio Press,
55 St. Thomas' Street, Oxford OX1 1JG,
by arrangement with Michael Joseph Ltd.

British Library Cataloguing in Publication Data

Poole, R. W. F.
    A backwoodsman's year.
    1. England. Rural regions. Social life – Biographies
    I. Title
    942.0858092

ISBN 1–85089–885–5

Printed and bound by Hartnolls, Bodmin, Cornwall
Cover designed by CGS Studios, Cheltenham

TO MY FAMILY:
a writer is not always a bundle of fun to live with

May

I am a Backwoodsman. What is a Backwoodsman? Backwoodsmen live their lives in remote areas of the country, from which they seldom emerge. You may sometimes encounter them in cities when they have occasion to visit their "Man of Business". You can recognise them by their high complexions and the smell of mothballs from the suit that was almost certainly their father's before them.

Backwoodsmen do not like cities: they suffer from claustrophobia and all the time are worrying about the stock and their dogs left at home. Their life lies down secret lanes and upon windswept hills: "Happy the man whose wish and care a few paternal acres bound." They like dogs, old friends, old clothes (and it has to be said) old Port.

Although they may become magistrates, sheriffs, and sit on endless local committees, Backwoodsmen shun the limelight. They regard politics rather in the same way as they regard golf and buggery: not really suitable pastimes for a gentleman. They may be just a little anachronistic and tend to conservatism with varying sizes of C. They have never heard of Sexism or Racism. They think "Abroad" is bloody and a place you only go in an Army tank. They regard death as part of a natural process. What do these strange shy creatures look like? They come in all shapes and sizes, but most of them have the sort of countenance that only a lifetime's exposure to wind, weather and whisky can properly achieve. Perhaps the following pages will help you recognise this noble breed should you happen on one of them unexpectedly.

Let us start on the first of May. I have come to regard the first of May as my new year. There are two main reasons for this: the first is that the hunting year starts on 1 May and for many years my life has been inextricably mixed with hunting; the second reason is that lambing has usually finished by this date and I can relax a trifle, let my belt out a notch, or two, and sleep of nights. May is a nice pottering month after some nine months' hard graft.

Spring is officially frowned upon in Northumberland. It is regarded as something effete and southern, like yuppies, barley barons, and women with bare feet and hairy legs. April can be a cruel month on the Borders, but May — well May may be different. Even in the wind-blasted, blue-fingered North there may come a whisper of rising sap, of burgeoning grass, of an increase in bird song. A morning will come when the wind blows soft on the cheek, and there is enough warmth in the sun to penetrate to the deep-frozen bone marrow. On such a morning the lambs lie quietly soaking up the energy from the sun, and the cloud shadows chase each other on the smooth green hills across the valley.

On such a morning a writer/shepherd will find some compelling reason for leaving his desk, gathering his dogs and his stick, and will deem it meet, right, and his bounden duty to do an extra round of the flock. After all, he will tell himself, a shepherd must always make time to look and to watch, and to notice the little things that may well have been missed in the hurly-burly of the early morning feeding run. To lean on one's stick in the warm spring sun is mightily pleasant, but to know that one is working and practising good husbandry by so doing gives the action extra spice.

Such an effort cannot be sustained indefinitely. It is hard to blame the writer/shepherd if he should halt on the rough bank above the quarry and seek the crafty little corner out of the wind which is well warmed by the morning sun, and where a rock fits snugly into the back. In fact, it would be a sin to waste appreciating such a spot on such a morning. While the collies roll and tumble in mock warfare on the bank, our man will probably get out his pipe and when it is firing nicely he will watch the changes of light and shade on the hills and the wheeling peewits. It is not for you to accuse him of idleness: he may well be thinking for all you know, for writers, and farmers, must think as well as scribble. I reckon that, in the circumstances, our man is making best use of the morning and that is all that one can ask of him.

My little farm is only sixty-five acres. When we moved to Northumberland it was my earnest intention to buy a proper farm: a hill farm for choice. Over three years we looked at several farms. Either they were too remote for my wife, or they required too much money spending on them, or the selling price was way beyond what they were worth. I was chary about borrowing too much money, and the way things have been going, I am glad that I was cautious. I had been renting a small block of land; it was old pasture and in poor fettle, but it was basically good stock land. It also had the most amazing view. I used to stand at the top of the big field below the wood and think what a wonderful place it would be to build a house. To cut short the story, two years later I bought the land and did just that, so here I am with my sixty-five acres and one of the finest views in England. A land agent told me that the view puts ten thousand pounds on the value of the house. I very much hope that his opinion will never have to be put to the test.

The farm is all grass and all sheep — some 240 mule ewes. Sheep are not as stupid as people think, but they are maddening, stubborn, greedy, and entail a lot of hard work. I suspect that if we keepers of sheep really costed out our time properly, we would find that we were just that — keepers of sheep; whereas we like to deceive ourselves that the sheep keep us. The trouble is that sheep are not just a job, they are a way of life, albeit a fairly pleasant one on the whole. Go to any gathering in this area, any public house, any dinner party, and at some stage the conversation will inevitably turn to sheep. Away the men will go with dogs and sticks, with louping ill, transit tetany, and vaginal prolapses; with baigies, neaps, and pot ale syrup; with Kelpies and Huntaways and Beardies. And their ladies will turn their eyes to Heaven and pray for deliverance. The wife of a friend (a London lady) says in suffering tones that whilst she has not yet learnt to talk about sheep she has learnt to listen about them.

Early May provides a breathing space after lambing. It is now a question of keeping the ewes full of milk and making sure that all the lambs are getting their rations; that they are not hanging themselves, drowning themselves, suffocating themselves, or whatever the latest fashion in self-immolation may be.

The ewes are still getting a daily ration of "cake". The feeding round is done before breakfast. Let us set out together this fine May morning.

I love the early mornings, and getting up is no hardship for me. The day starts with the shipping forecast. I want to hear what Tyne is likely to get up to, to tell myself the ritual joke about the German Bight being done by Dogger, and to think how fortunate I am not to farm in Rockall or south-east Iceland. Then it is getting up to the news headlines; shaving and abluting to the farming programme and tying my boot laces to Prayer for the Day.

The yard is a square. The house forms one side, the stables another. The sheep shed is opposite the house. The wood completes the square. The ground slopes away in front of the house, to the west, down to the Powburn. On the other side of the valley the Cheviots roll away: Fawden, Hedgehope, The Cunyans, Shilmoor, and a peeping corner of the great Cheviot itself. No man could tire of this view, for not only is it different each and every day with changes of light and shade and colour, but it often changes by the hour. The air off the hills is a potent draught that has gathered salt off the Irish Sea and has then swept across 100 miles of heather, bracken and bent grass to fill my lungs, and make me cough with the strength of it.

It is time to meet the sheep dogs who will figure largely in this book and who are as much a part of my daily life as Filofax and season ticket are for others. There are two dogs.

Wizz, the collie bitch, I bought for a bottle of whisky when she was a whelp; her large attendant louse population was thrown in free. She is brilliant, lazy, greedy and sagacious; and at times totally maddening.

Then there is Oz. Oz is not a collie at all. He is a Kelpie, an Australian sheep dog. They are called Kelpies because they all go back to a bitch called Kelpie who emigrated from the west of Scotland just prior to 1870. They are small, smooth-coated dogs with prick ears, and they come in either red or black. And they bark, St Australasius how they do bark; and this shifts the sheep. In theory, they bark when you tell them to and stop when you say, "Quiet". But, as in so many things, theory does not always accord with practice. Sometimes you have to say, "Shut up!"; sometimes "B—— well shut up!"; and sometimes, "SHUTUPFORFUCKSAKEYOU-BLOODYREDAUSTRALIANBASTARD!!!". From this, you will have gathered that Oz is an enthusiast. He loves his work and asks no more from life than to be allowed to work sheep all day and every day. He is also a dog of immense charm.

After I have loosed the collies, I cross to the shed for the ATV; yes, I thought you might ask that. An All Terrain Vehicle is basically a four-wheeled motorbike with large low ground pressure tyres. It has ten forward gears and drives on all four wheels. It will carry you and a reasonable load over the steepest, roughest and wettest ground that you can imagine. It will go where a horse cannot. It will pull a small trailer (say half a ton), spread fertiliser, spray, and cut grass. It has been described as the biggest advance in sheep farming since the collie dog, and I would go along with that. Mine is called Rupert, and if you want to know why, I'm not going to tell you.

As soon as I start the engine, there comes from the field a rising chorus of complaint about the appalling slackness and sloth of the service: a sort of ovine "Why are we waiting". We talk of people being like sheep; by the same token sheep are very like people.

The bike is loaded and off we go. From all round the field sheep come hurrying, trailing clouds of scurrying lambs. Sheep have no table manners, and will trample anything to get at the food. A good mule ewe weighs about 150lbs. If you have eight of them swirling around your legs, all mad for the bag you are carrying, you may experience difficulties (a) in moving, (b) in standing upright at all. However, that worries me not at all for this is where Oz comes in. He confronts the multitude and harangues them. He points out their shortcomings and deficiency of personal charm in a flow of lurid Antipodean language so foul that even the most hardened six-crop ewe bridles and blushes a bit. Anything four-legged that still does not take the hint gets nipped on the nose by Wizz. By these means I can pursue the even tenor of my ways, shaking out a line of cobs onto the ground without being molested.

Whilst the ewes are gobbling, I check the lambs. A big pack of them are rioting up and down the hedgeback, chasing and twisting and turning. I do not worry too much about them; a playing lamb is a happy, healthy lamb. It is the non players that I look closely at. I look for scour. May is the prime month for the dreaded nematode worm which kills little lambs. The first sign of anything "skittered" and it is time to reach for the drenching gun. If a lamb with a cloudy eye is left, the eye may well ulcerate and die. It must be treated — but First Catch Your Lamb. The crook on a "lambing stick" is so shaped that it will fit neatly round the front of a lamb, enabling it to be retrieved and neatly fielded with the other hand — but you have to be quick. Lambs are very fast and agile, which no one has ever accused me of being. The trick is to keep one's eye on the lamb: it is no good closing one's eye and swiping hopefully; that is how I played tennis on the first and last occasion that I attempted that very moderate game. The cap-tured lamb is placed firmly between the knees where it wriggles and complains vigorously. Aureomycin powder is the answer to cloudy eyes and I always carry a puffer pack in my pocket. Indeed there is a small veterinary box on the back of the ATV which contains hypodermic syringes, penicillin, calcium boroglutinate, antibiotic spray; first aid for most conditions.

The feeding and checking over, I have a ride round the boundaries of the field to check all the places where a sickly lamb might lie up, and the trouble spots where a lamb might get into difficulties. Then back to the shed, load up again and off to the next lot of ewes and lambs.

It takes me about an hour and a half to feed round at this time of year. On a fine May morning, it is a very pleasing job. Quite the opposite to the drear, dour mornings when the easterly wind brings in the dank, cold fret off the North Sea.

When I come back into the yard for the last time, the nostrils twitch to the smell of bacon; if there is a nicer smell after a couple of hours in the fresh air, then I do not know it.

Breakfast is a very important meal for me: it must never be rushed, and should take at least an hour. First of all, the bacon and eggs (and maybe a sausage, or possibly a bit of black pudding), tea and toast are quickly despatched. Then comes the important time. The feet go up on the stool, another of several cups of strong tea is poured and the pipe is lit. The after-breakfast pipe is the most important one of the day. This is the moment when all the systems are put in full working order. The day's work-schedule is gone through and thought out. Plans are made or altered. It is the Board Meeting, the Editorial Conference, Mental Muster Parade, call it what you will, but whatever you call it, it is a vital part of my day and is never lightly abandoned.

After breakfast, what then? I have three jobs: farming, writing, and hunting. Between the three of them I work seven days a week, and sometimes eight. This is no hardship because I love my work, and a change of work is the best relaxation. I do have a week's holiday every year because my wife insists on it, but I am thoroughly bored after forty-eight hours. We will come to the Holiday in due process of time. Just for now, I think we will do a little hunting.

At this point I hear someone say that, being May, they thought that the hunting season was over. That is correct, of course, but the work goes on. It is not possible just to wrap hounds up in tissue paper and put them away in a cupboard until the next hunting season.

For some twenty years, when I was hunting hounds, I used to go to the kennels every day. Indeed for many years I lived at the kennels and the hounds were my whole life, as they must be to a huntsman. The fox-hound is a truly remarkable animal. There is no animal that I have loved as long or as deeply, and they have rewarded me by returning that love and by knocking their guts out for me in the hunting field.

There is a great mental link between a good hunts-man and his hounds: an empathy, a symbiosis, call it what you will. Throughout the hunting world it is called "the thread", which I think describes it as well as anything.

To weave "the thread" you have to be a "dog" man, and hounds know instantly whether you are one or not. If you are not, they will never do any good for you. Dogginess is the first essential ingredient that makes a huntsman, but there is more, much more. The next ingredient is time. You have to spend time with your hounds and gain their respect and their love.

Hounds should be out of the kennels as much as possible in the summer. They do not like being shut up all the time any more than you would. Very few hunts can afford the large staff of yesteryear when there might well have been five, or six, men in the kennels, and possibly twenty in the stables. One or two full-time hunt servants would be nearer the modern norm, and they simply do not have the time that the old men did. Even so, hounds should go out twice a day. Some hunts are blessed with lovely "grass yards". These are wired-in enclosures where the hounds can be turned out on a nice day. They are *not* a substitute for exercise, but if the weather is fine hounds are just as well out there in between times, galloping and playing, or just soaking up the sun. One hunt I was with had a lovely grass yard of about three acres dotted with old chestnut trees. On hot summer afternoons I used to sling my hammock in the trees and hounds used to come and lie underneath and we all used to snooze in the shade.

The day starts early in a hunt kennels. The first chore is washing down, for cleanliness is a religion with all good hunt servants. By seven o'clock, the yards and the lodges (bedrooms) are as clean and shining as many gallons of water and vigorous work with a bass broom can make them. Then it is time for walkies and hounds greet the moment with enthusiasm, but first there is the coupling up to be done.

Foxhound puppies are usually born in March, April or May. Aged nine or ten weeks they "go out to walk".

They go away to farms or shepherd's steadings where they receive the sort of individual attention and freedom that it would not be possible to give them in the kennels. They roam free amongst ducks, hens, dogs and sheep. They get their ears boxed by the farm cat; they go out with the collies and learn to ignore sheep and cattle; they tear the washing from the line and steal the joint from the kitchen table. They are loved, cursed, petted and chastised as necessary. All crime about the farm is attributed to "yon bloody puppy". I do not know why anyone walks a hound puppy but they do, year after year, and generation after generation.

At last the puppy will outgrow childhood. It will start to wander; it will start to hunt, or will follow parties of hikers and have to be retrieved from some distant police station. Now about one year old, it is time for it to return to the kennels and start the next stage of its education. It now has to learn good order and discipline. The first stage of this is for the tyro to be coupled to an old hound. Couples are simply two collars with a length of chain in between. Where old Gaffer goes, there goes Tyro also.

When the time comes for "Walking Out", the kennel gates are thrown open. Let there be no unseemly rush: that would be bad manners. The huntsman will stand outside the open gate whilst hounds wait politely inside for the trigger word that lets them through. A quicksilver mass of black, white, lemon and tan; waving sterns, grinning faces, they jostle and cavort around the huntsman eager to be off. At the road gate, another pause. "Hold up" is the command, while the whipper-in scouts the road. It is 0710, the Flying Roadman is due past on his way to work, but is late again. Here he comes: *vroom*, a toot, a wave, and a cloud of exhaust fumes to make hounds sneeze and that is him out of the way. Round the bend, the lane stretches straight with wide grassy verges. "Trot on" says the huntsman. Hounds have been clustered around him up until now but the trigger word frees them. They surge forward, galloping, leaping, rolling each other over in mock combat, laughing and playing. The young and eager race each other down the road, whilst the older ones who know it all walk sedately about the huntsman.

"Gently now" and the front runners turn and come racing back to the main body.

"Y-o-t-e" calls the whipper-in and everyone stops. Old Gaffer is vomiting and heaves up the wad of medicinal grasses that he has eaten. It is a good time to let everyone have a pick out of the long grass in the hedgeback. It is a "grass morning". On certain mornings, the springing grasses have powerful emetic and cleansing properties: nature's alka seltzer, if you like. Hounds must always be given the opportunity to make use of this.

"Statesman looks pretty sound now."

"Aye, it was a nasty cut that, but it's healed now. Here Statesman, lad, let's have a look at your foot. Now what are you grumbling about, you old fool; you know I'm not going to hurt you. It was a nasty cut right enough."

"Here old dog, Statesman; have a biscuit and stop grumbling. Statesman I said. Your name's not Statesman, Gifted; what have you done to deserve a biscuit? Go on then, catch it."

"Gently Ravager; come out of there."

"All finished with the grass? Come on then, dears, let's be on."

The lane drops down through a little copse with its early lacework of new leaf to a three-cross road with a grass triangle. A well-mannered pack of hounds should go happily along the road in front of their huntsman, and should be waiting politely for him at any road junction they happen to come across. Today we will turn to the right and through the field gate at the end of the copse. Hounds spread out as they enter the field. The old hounds will be seeking all the myriad of strange and wonderful smells that a hound's nose can take on board. Sometimes you can feel the thrill run through them like an electric current, perhaps as they touch an overnight fox line. They have to be gently reminded that the season is over. The younger hounds are galloping and playing, leaping and rolling in the dewy grass. One will suddenly decide to be the clown and will set off twisting and turning, chased by an ever growing tail of pursuers. At the other end of the field, a flap of ewes and lambs gather together at the approach of what appears to them to be a pack of potential aggressors. The whipper-in goes quietly up on the outside of the loosely grouped hounds. Of all the crimes that a hound can commit, chasing a sheep is the greatest. A young hound who does it once receives a summary and memorable thrashing. A second offence is a capital crime. It is just too serious a matter to take a chance on. Hounds are taken regularly through all sorts of stock and are presented with all sorts of temptation during the summer: they cannot learn about what they never see. Today, the sheep are passed and properly ignored.

The river is always a favourite spot to pause, especially on a nice warm morning. Hounds love playing in the water, and swimming after a judiciously thrown biscuit.

A rabbit explodes from a gorse bush and a couple of young hounds set off in hysterical pursuit, which is sharply interdicted by the whipper-in. They return shame-faced to the huntsman.

"Shame on you, the pair of you." He takes the ring-leader by the loose skin under the jaw and gently shakes the hound's head repeating, "War riot, war riot" — ryot being old English for rabbit.

That will do for this fine May morning. We will wander back up the steep stony track to the kennels with the sun falling warmly on the back and the first trickle of sweat running down the spine.

We have already briefly mentioned the Merry Nematode. These jolly little things live in the intestines of sheep. They do not bother mature sheep much, but they can kill little lambs. In May, the flockmaster (which is an upmarket name for sheep farmer) goes for his dosing gun and zaps the sneaky nematode. This means the first gather of the summer. The ewes and lambs are usually left undisturbed until the lambs are at least a month old. In the course of this month, the maternal bond should become unbreakable. It can be a bit tenuous in the early stages and has to be reinforced by regular "mothering up" to make sure that each ewe has her own allotted lambs with her. Any waifs have to be restored to the maternal fold and reacceptance super-vised. The presence of a collie dog reinforces the ewe's maternal instincts. At a month to six weeks, the maternal bond is reckoned to be sound enough to stand up to the confusion of a gather.

First gather your sheep. The first gather has its problems, mainly the lambs. The ewes will have been through the pens many times, the lambs never. There will be confusion. There will be about 100 ewes and 200 lambs in each "cut" of sheep. Frantic lambs will be separated from their mothers; distressed mothers will be calling for their lambs. The noise will be tremendous. The problem is getting the whole swirling mass moving in the right direction. The lambs are convinced that mother is somewhere back in the field, and the ewes are convinced that the children have been left behind. The only thing that gets the show moving forward is even more noise behind it. Border collies do not bark on the whole, so this is where Oz comes into his own. Driving sheep is Oz's idea of heaven. He is tireless. First he runs to the head of the column and barks to move them forward; he then returns all the way down the side, barking all the way. Then round the back, then up to the front again, still barking and always at a hand-gallop. I have seen him do this for two hours at a stretch when I have had sheep on the road. He can certainly shift sheep.

The crucial moment is the entrance to the yard. The lambs are twisting and turning, desperate to double back. If anything does manage to break back at this point, we could be in trouble. Fred and I re-double the shouting and the flapping of the arms. The bleating increases. The dogs fling themselves from side to side, fielding the jibbers. Then the happy moment when the gate is swung shut; the sheep are enclosed and Fred and I can lean on the gate, mop our brows and say something which more or less approximates to "Allelujah!" Oz finds a bit of shade to pant in. Wizz has a better idea, she goes straight to the nearest water trough and lies in that with just her grinning head sticking out.

I do not employ anyone on my little farm, but Fred and Tom usually come in to help out on big handling days. They are contract shepherds, or as they say up here, "working loose".

A sheep handling operation can be compared to an hour glass, with the holding pens at one end from which the sheep go in single file through a "race" to another set of holding pens. There are many variations but that is the basic idea.

The first thing is to "shed" the lambs off into a separate pen, which has to be done carefully as they are still small enough not to be improved by being trampled on. Once they are separated, we deal first with the ewes. They are just in for a worm drench; they file through the race and receive their blessing as they go.

The lambs are different. They are going to get an injection as well. Amongst the many forms of illness which sheep enjoy, the Clostridium infections loom large. They have jolly-sounding names like "Braxy", "Blackleg", "Pulpy Kidney", and "Struck", but they are all lethal.

We work three handed. One catches and holds the lambs. One sticks the worm dose down the throat. The third member of the team sticks in the needle. Thus is each lamb doubly blessed and released to seek its mother amongst the milling group of anxious matrons who are urgently demanding the return of their off-spring. The job develops a rhythm of its own: grab, dose, jag; grab, dose, jag. It will continue at this steady pace throughout the day, broken only by pauses for taking away one lot of sheep and bringing in another — and of course for meals. Never for one moment let us underestimate the importance of meals. You will come to realise that meals loom large in the life of your average, run of the mill, Backwoodsman.

By teatime, the job should be nearing completion. We shall be glad to finish although it is by no means an unpleasant day's work. There is a certain satisfaction from working with sheep, and if you do not get that then you should not work with them. Nor should you think that the day passes in stony silence. Fred, Tom and I are used to working together; we are at ease together. The day's graft is leavened with a certain amount of humour and what I have heard described as "rough badinage"; at least, I think that is what it is. There is also the local gossip to be kept flowing. Gossip is like water: it is better on the move, changing, widening and deepening as it goes. Whatever you do, keep it flowing onwards and away from yourself.

There is always a last lamb, and it is a gladsome sight for men and dogs now grown weary. It is also the occasion for a little verbal ritual:

"That's the last," says Fred.

"That's the one we should have started with," says Tom.

"Allelujah!" says I. It is right to praise the Lord for a job well done.

June

June is a social month when the Backwoodsman may occasionally issue forth from his lonely fissure in the hills and try to establish some tentative form of contact with what we will refer to as the "Human Race" for want of a better cliché.

On the first Tuesday in June you will nearly always find me in London. This is when the Annual General Meeting of the Masters of Foxhounds Association is held and is as good an excuse as any for patting the wife on the head, telling her to be a good girl, and setting off for some modest junketing in the Great Wen. I would hate to live in London and I am always glad to leave it, but I quite look forward to my occasional brief visits.

I stay at The Club. It is neither the greatest nor the least of the Gentlemen's Clubs but it provides a pleasant oasis where I can browse, sluice and lay my head, at what must be very reasonable prices by London standards.

My London day follows a fairly immutable regime. After breakfast I set out for Jermyn Street to do my shopping for the annual shirt, for it is only here that those whose collar size approximates to the average waist measurement can get themselves kitted out.

Then there is the haircut.

Then there is an hour in Hatchards.

Then it is nearly time for luncheon.

If you were to stand outside a certain well-known building, in a certain well-known street, on this particular Tuesday in June, you might well be struck by the thought that the stream of men you saw entering the building all conformed to a certain type. They would all be dressed in dark suits of good cut but allowing not the slightest concession to any modern fashion. The other common factor you might notice would be the sort of complexions that can only be produced by thirty years continous exposure to wind, weather and whisky. The masters are going to luncheon.

It is a jolly occasion. There will be a lot of old friends who may not have been seen for a year, and whose increased avoirdupois will have to be compared unfavourably to one's own sylphlike figure. There will be the usual rumours to be confirmed, denied and embroidered. A few saunters down memory lane. A little quiet character mugging to be undertaken. A jolly good gossip all round, in fact, and some passable scoff to be well washed down. Then a glass of port whilst a Very Senior Foxhunter says a few (mercifully) brief, and (hopefully) well chosen words. Another Very Senior Foxhunter will then tell a story which will be very funny, but not the sort that would go down well with the local Women's Institute. Then it is time for the meeting.

At one time, the meeting used to happen in the same place as the luncheon which was handy, but we moved when they started pricing the meal in petrodollars. So now we have to walk a quarter of a mile which is a horrible bore but with a bit of luck there may be someone I know with a limousine waiting. It is amazing how many MsFH you can get in the back of a Bentley: perhaps there ought to be a national competition.

The meeting takes place at a premier hotel. The masters are an anachronism. They are probably the only people in the hotel not dressed in flowing robes and burnouses. The staff regard us with grave suspicion: we do not smell of oil.

I suppose that you all want a blow by blow account of what happens at the meeting, but you cannot have it because (a) it is confidential, and (b) I usually sleep through the entire proceedings. I do have an arrangement with my friend Mackenzie, whose ample form usually buttresses me on the left, to poke me in the ribs at any key moments. I am programmed to say "here, here" without properly disturbing my siesta.

Sometimes a few of us get together for a little gentle dinner in the evening. Evenings always have to end and sometimes they end one way, and sometimes another. This particular evening was ending with the intake of a little restorative whisky, which was necessary to combat the effects of the not inconsiderable amount of wine that had been consumed previously. The talk was of a particularly high order — I think we had got on to the fascinating subject as to whether if Belvoir Dexter '95 had indeed bonked all the bitches he was shown on paper as having bonked, would he have had (a) the strength, and (b) the time ever to go hunting: pretty high flown stuff.

We were ignoring the Colonel who kept leaping out from behind a marble pillar and asking if anyone wanted to fight. A disagreement had been rumbling all evening, and now came to a head. The Captain was concerned because he felt that his next door neighbour, the Major, was trying to seduce his (the Captain's) very rich lady joint master. I should point out in fairness to all parties that the implications were entirely financial, and no sexual impropriety was being mooted; well, not much anyway. The matter now came to flashpoint.

The Major leaped to his feet and suggested that if the Captain did not keep his long pointed nose out of other people's business, other people just might rearrange its shape.

The Captain rose to his feet to reply. He was sadly unmindful of the fact that he was without benefit of braces and his curvature was unhelpful for keeping trousers in their proper place. His trousers fell down.

The Major turned to stamp off in high dudgeon.

The Colonel, who had been sulking behind his pillar, felt that his time had come at last and leaped out, calling upon the Major to "put his fists up". Without pausing, the Major just stuck a large flat hand into the Colonel's face which set him swinging giddily round his pillar. We all went out to wave goodbye to the Major.

The Captain's trousers fell down again.

Summer is the time when Masters of Hounds go visiting. Let us just consider for a moment how hunting works. Hunting takes place almost entirely on privately-owned land. The hunt has no right to cross any of that land; it does so only with the permission and blessing of the farmers. I never cease to marvel at the fact that the vast majority of British farmers continue to welcome the local hunt, even though things are far from easy in the agricultural industry.

To foster and maintain this good will, the sensible Master of Hounds will spend a great deal of time on public relations. Most farmers and landowners like a social call from the Master. Even amongst farmers who are not enthusiastic about hunting, it will be counted unto him/her for righteousness.

Some hunts will have a thousand to fifteen hundred farms within their boundaries and ideally they should all be visited every year, but that is impossible for one person to achieve, hence the need for joint masters these days.

Let us now set out on a round of farm visits and see what the day brings forth.

One of the first rules is never to be in a hurry. The most number of visits I have ever managed in a day is fifteen and I felt quite ill at the end of it for reasons which will become clear. Most farmers are hospitable people and most are pleased to receive a visit from the Master; an offer of hospitality would be the norm and should not be refused. The trouble is that hospitality comes in different shapes and sizes. In the course of a day of farm visiting, you may be presented with tea, coffee, home-made wine, home-made cider, sweet sherry, whisky, gin, rum, cake, biscuits, buns, pie, a three-course dinner, coffee, tea, and port wine. In no case will the Master wish to give offence by refusing, but by now the cause of possible illness may have become much clearer.

Old Jim, now sadly deceased, was a lovely man and a desperately keen hunting farmer. He was also a great raconteur and a thesaurus of local knowledge. I used to look forward to the prospect of visiting him with mixed feelings. I would have to go in for the inevitable "quick one". The trouble was that it was never one and they were never quick. "They" were whisky, and they used to come in half-pint tumblers. In spite of having a drop of water with them, they were still the colour of old mahogany. That would loosen our tongues, and conversation would concentrate on hunting, farming, racing, shepherding, and drinking. There was always another "eye to be wetted", always yet another half to be had.

The great problem with visiting Jim was (a) getting

away, and (b) getting home. There was the infamous time when one of Jim's sons had to deliver me home laid out in the back of the farm's pick-up truck. He was a lovely man for all that.

Perce was another problem. Perce was actually a problem I encountered when I lived and hunted in the West of England, but I cannot bear to leave him out. Perce had been "in service" and had been set up in his farm by a local nobleman, Lord X. Perce made cider. Many farms in the West of England make their own cider; the product ranges from the Absolutely Scrumptious to the Quite Unbelievably Filthy. Perce's cider did not even aspire to the last category and I used to dread going there. I suppose Perce did some active farming, but whenever I arrived at his farm, he was always standing in the middle of the yard leaning lightly on a prong (pitch fork). As soon as he saw me, he would perk up and greet me warmly. Then he would lug the huge watch out of his waistcoat pocket and say: "Well, as Lord X used to say, 'It's time for a wet.'"

The cider house lurked in a corner of the yard. I always felt that there should have been a sign above the door: "All hope abandon ye who enter here". The cider shed was a long dark lean-to. Down the back wall was a row of barrels. Above the barrels, festooned in innumerable cobwebs and encrusted with rat droppings, was a shelf. On the shelf were two china mugs; they celebrated the coronation of George V. Since then they had seen much service and little or no soap and water. They were chipped and cracked, and the cracks were sealed with the grime of ages. With due ceremony Perce used to take down the mugs, blow the dust out of them, and give them a polish with a handkerchief which had obviously been doing good general farm work.

"Now, Master, just you try a drop of this." One of the nice things about good cider is how it captures all the bright colours of autumn in its pellucid depths. You can taste the summer, the harvest home, the hot hay fields; they are all there in the apples which have poured their goodness into the drink. There was not much of that stupid nonsense about Perce's cider. The first searing sip took the roof off the mouth and continued stripping all the way down to the stomach, where a chemical reaction of intense ferocity at once began, as the innocent internal organs made a strong formal protest. But that was not all. Good cider looks good. Perce's brew was green and opaque. There was a sort of slimy weed floating on the top. Below the surface, nameless things floated and bubbled. Because the mugs were china, one was mercifully spared the trauma of seeing what they were.

"Lovely drop of stuff, that," Perce would say, smacking his lips, and giving them a quick wipe with The Handkerchief. "Now let's just try this yere barrel. 'Tis a drop of that good stuff you liked last year . . ."

In June there is clipping of sheep which is done for two good reasons: health and profit.

Health because *you* would not like to be running about in the summer heat wearing your winter overcoat. It would become sweaty, nasty and verminous. That may be all right for you, but I do not want it for my sheep. The fleece is also worth something, not a lot, but a bit. If only the Urban Person would realise how much healthier and more attractive he/she would be in natural fibres instead of all those perfectly frightful 'lons and 'lenes. Man-made fibres just make people sweat and accentuate the enormous size of their over-fed bums and beer bellies. Wear more wool and feel more healthy — you'll also help to make me wealthy.

In the old days clipping would have been a social occasion. When Jack at Seven Sikes clipped, all the neighbours would come over and lend a hand, and at the end of the day a huge supper would be laid on in the house. Thus would each farm in turn be dealt with. With the depopulation of the hills, this custom has largely fallen into desuetude. Some people still do their own clipping; getting in a few sheep at a time and doing them themselves. I know a farm where they still clip with the old hand shears. Most people now use teams of professional shearers, often New Zealanders. A top class professional shearer might clip 300 sheep in a day at something like 50p a sheep — and I reckon that he earns every penny he gets.

It is not a job I relish. It is a long, sweaty, boring and trying day. In fact, I do not join in the clipping myself, using my bad back as an excuse, and anyway it is best done by skilled practitioners who enjoy the work. It is a skill that has to be acquired when one is young and supple and the body can get accustomed to the contortions necessary for clipping sheep. Bobby and Robin do my clipping; for two months of the year they do nothing but clip. They have a home-made trailer built on a caravan chassis which they tow from farm to farm. One side of the trailer lets down to form a flat platform on which the clippers stand. The other side of the trailer consists of a long narrow passage where the sheep stand before being dragged onto the platform through springloaded swing gates. The electric clipping machines hang on their individual gallows at each end of the platform.

Apart from the two star performers, there will be a full supporting cast for the day. There is the wrapper: as the completed fleece is kicked to one side by the clipper, the wrapper seizes it, folds it in a specific and rather complicated way and rolls it up. In the old days he would then twist out a wool rope and bind the roll; you could play rugger with a well-tied fleece. The Wool Marketing Board no longer like tied fleeces so they are just rolled and popped straight into a huge hessian bag called a sheet. There has to be another body standing inside the sheet (it is hung up) packing the fleeces tightly.

Meanwhile, stage left, there will be the "pusher upper". It is his job to see that the catching-pen at the back of the trailer is always full of sheep so he has a gangway, and a holding-pen full of sheep. Ah, but how does he get them into his holding-pen? That is where the dogs and I come in. As many sheep as possible are held in the shed overnight. This means that in the morning they will be dry of the fleece and empty of belly; both prerequisites for clipping. First thing in the morning, the lambs (who take no part in the proceedings) are separated from their mothers, and the shed becomes hideous with protest.

By 0700 we shall have made a start. The catching-pen will be full. Each shearer goes in, catches a sheep, "cowps" it (turns it upside down, which you do with one hand, if you know how) and backs out through the spring gate with the customer. I imagine that it is something like a ladies' crimping centre: the ewe sits up on its bottom and is held by skilful use of the knees and one hand. Down the neck go the clippers, down the belly, down the legs, along the side, turn over, along the other side, down the back and over the tail. Hey presto, a surprised and naked-looking ewe scrambles to her feet and heads for the open shed door in stiff-legged bounds. Her "jacket" is kicked to one side for the wrapper. A pull of the cord switches off the clipping machine. A quick wipe of the brow and back into the catching-pen for the next customer.

So it goes throughout the day. Bait at ten o'clock. Dinner at twelve. Tea at five. It will quite likely be a sixteen-hour day by the time we finish. A hard day but I would not have you think that it is a day of sour grind. There will be a leaven of highly intellectual conversation: how to whistle through fingers covered in sheep shit; how many litters of fox cubs there are about this year; that sort of thing. Bobby is also a great raconteur. No, I really must not. Are you really sure that you want to hear one? Very well, but I will be a little circumspect in my choice.

A new teacher comes to a school deep in the Border hills. The first thing she does is to clear out from her desk some of the rubbish her predecessor has left behind, and then sets off to find somewhere to tip the detritus. In the passage she meets a small boy.

"Hello," she says, "where's the bin?"

"Ah've bin for a piss. Where's thoo gannin'?"

That, as they say, is quite enough of that.

★   ★   ★

By June the foxhound whelps will be old enough to go out to walk; ten to twelve weeks being the norm. Puppies need space, therefore most puppy walkers tend to be farmers, shepherds, or some such. I do remember a puppy actually being walked in a post office in the middle of a country town; it used to sleep quite happily in the sorting office. All was fine until it ate the bookmaker's list one morning and the local betting shop was thrown into confusion.

Puppy walkers may be divided into two categories: those who take a puppy every year without question and those who are never under any circumstances going to walk a puppy again — not until it arrives, that is. You have to understand that a ten-week-old foxhound puppy is one of the most pathetic, endearing, wide-eyed, maternal-instinct-provoking bundles of skin and unco-ordinated legs that has ever been invented. It looks as though it ought to have a key sticking out of its back. At that age there is as yet no hint of the boisterous, thieving, maddening rogue which will develop.

Let us set off one fine June day with a box in the back of the Land Rover containing a selection of the wares. The first call is up the valley to Greensike Hill. There will be no customer resistance here; in fact, it is a bespoke order. It must be a bitch and it must be a lineal descendant of old Gracious who was the first puppy walked on the farm twenty-five years before.

There is no need to hesitate: puppy under arm, it is straight into the kitchen and plonk it down in the middle of the kitchen floor where it promptly widdles with nerves at this strange and frightening place. The old half-blind collie gets stiffly from its place by the Rayburn and comes across to sniff at the newcomer. Fifteen years ago the old collie and this puppy's great-grandmother were puppies together and rejoiced accordingly. The old dog knows that in a few days time he will be having his tail pulled, his ears chewed, and his patience sorely tried by this sad-looking little creature, who is now widdling again.

Whilst I get a cup of tea and a slice of cake, the puppy is whisked up to be made a fuss of on the sofa where it will spend a great deal of time in the next nine months, resting between bouts of lawlessness.

The next call requires a little more cunning. You will have noted that I stopped for a cup of tea at the first call. This means that the next call will take place after tea when the children are sure to be home from school. The next call is a "Never — another — puppy — as — long — as — I — live — Isn't — that — right — John" place. Mavis says this every year. John, sensible married man that he is, never says anything. Indeed, the moment he sees the truck coming through the gate, he will be on his bike and away to the farthest possible corner of the hill where he will sit and smoke his pipe and wait for the all clear to sound.

Mavis goes straight for the jugular. She hopes that I have not come to try and persuade her to have another puppy; not after the last one, and it is no good my thinking that I can get round her, so there.

I use a forearm block. No thought of asking her to have a puppy; just called in to scrounge a spot of tea because I knew it was her baking day. My perfidy knows no bounds. Mavis's baking is justly famous. She is down for a pinfall. I eat several slices of delicious cake and we gossip — Mavis's gossip is almost as good as her cake. Puppies are never mentioned, but all the time I have one ear cocked for childish noises-off. I look covertly at my watch. I reckon about 50 seconds to the end of the round: 20-19-18-17-

"Mam, can we have this one?" The big dog puppy is cradled in Mary's arms. He and Craig are licking each other's noses, and little Ian is helping it to wag its stern. Mavis goes a deep purply colour, but the explosion is defused by a chorus of *"Please,* Mams." I put down my tea cup: time for the rabbit punch.

"Of course, if you had two they would be much less trouble; keep each other amused."

"Oooh yes, Mam, can we have two? There's a brill little black one. Can we have it, Mam? *Please,* Mam; *please* Mam." 9-10-*out*! Mavis is flat on the canvas. It is time to flap the towel in her face.

"I must say, it's jolly sporting of you, Mavis."

"You bugger," says Mavis. There is only one thing that I can do in the circumstances. Mere words would be superfluous. I have another piece of cake.

There is a most tiresome intrusion into the steady mooch of my life during June: the Holiday. I see no reason for the Holiday. I do not agree with those who say that my life is one big holiday, but I do enjoy my work. Nevertheless Head Office decrees that there shall be a holiday, so a holiday is what there is. It is now established that I am unable to stand the strain of the traditional holiday for more than a week. I do not want you to think that Susie and I spend long winter evenings poring over glossy travel brochures and agonising over which sun-blessed, sea-kissed resort shall receive our patronage. The holiday destination is like the law of the Medes and Persians; it changeth not. We go and stay with my mother. I know that, by convention, all writers' mothers should live in a back street in Bolton with a cat, a bottle of Elliman's Embrocation and an outside netty. I must profusely apologise to you all for mother's shortcomings, but she will insist on living in Spain. The trouble is that she lives in the wrong part of Spain. To get to her, it is necessary to fly to either Alicante or Valencia. If those two names do not strike fear and loathing into the mind then you have had little experience of travelling to southern Spain in the summer months: especially by Charter Flights Ltd.

Charter Flights Ltd work on the basis that all their passengers probably have criminal tendencies and have a collective IQ of 35 (per aircraft load). They like their paying customers to assemble in good time; like twelve hours before take off. Each passenger is then strip-searched and escorted to the special departure lounge which is tastefully surrounded with electrified barbed wire and hungry-looking Dobermann dogs. Charter companies obviously go to great lengths to find the right sort of staff to get your holiday off to a good start: many of them are graduates of Mississippi State Correctional Institution. All this, of course, brings out the best amongst your fellow travellers, especially if you are lucky enough to share a plane with the Mary and Geordie 18-30 Club. The English do not feel comfortable being comfortable. A little adversity brings out the best in the national character, and also gives an excuse for sinking terrifying quantities of rum and pep, and Newcastle Brown Ale before take off. A lot of this may well be returned to the light of day before you are all into the twenty-fourth in-flight rendering of "Here we go, Here we go, Here we go!" or, as it might be, "Viva España!"

The problems do not end even at Alicante where the Holiday Tour reps will refuse to believe that there is such a thing as an independent traveller and will be intent on forcing you aboard one of their luxury coaches complete with barred windows. However, I make sure that the Mammy is there and that she will have a mobile squad of the Guardia Civil with her to extract us.

I have to admit that after the flight things improve. Mother used to live on the coast outside a little town. The little town is now a vast sprawl of gimcrack villas and is thronged with Germans, French, Swedes, Dutch and British, all displaying unsightly fish-white northern thighs and sagging beer bellies and yelling at the top of their voices. There was a brief stir of excitement one summer when there was a reported sighting of a genuine Spaniard somewhere in the town, but this was later dismissed as rumour.

Mother had the sense to see the change coming and she bought a derelict farmhouse outside a tiny village far back in the mountains. This is now a place of enchantment. Mother is the only foreigner in the place and the village has enfolded her in its vast collective bosom. Even a walk up to get the bread involves endless hand shakings and conversation and embracings.

The village sits in a hollow surrounded by its olive, orange, and almond groves which extend up the mountains in ever more improbable terraces. From the front of the house you can look down the valley and glimpse the distant sea.

It is only when you go to somewhere like this that you realise what a silent place our country is becoming. The Spanish mountainside is indeed "bee loud" and strident with grasshoppers. There are massed flights of butterflies and the rough bits between the terraces abound with wild flowers. In England our "progressive" methods have all but done for these things. Although I have no sprays on my farm, there are few flowers, few bees, no grasshoppers, and even butterflies rarely come to the thistle patch that I always keep for them. Terrible damage has been done that cannot be reversed.

The mountain is a mass of bird life. My favourites are the golden orioles and the hoopoes. Kites wheel in the thermals. At night I have counted six different nightingales all singing at once. However, there is a reverse side to the conservation coin for the Spanish are great shooters. Every Sunday, war breaks out on the mountain; if it flies or moves, the Spaniards will shoot at it.

It is my contention that country people are much the same all over the world. Go into any village in Spain, France, or even America if it comes to that, and you will find people who have exact counterparts in Toller Porcorum or Barton le Coggles. Electo, who is mother's chief adviser in the village, is a dead ringer for a chap I grew up alongside in Cornwall. I go down and practise my fractured Spanish on Electo and drink his wine — which I have to say is something of an acquired taste. His daughter learns English at school and can usually get as far as "Good morning" before she is consumed with shyness. Serafina, the wife, has adopted Mother and continually appears on her doorstep with baskets of fruit, or jars of delicious honey. They are immensely kind.

I sometimes wonder whether we would react as well to foreigners who plonked themselves down in our midst at home. It has to be said that there is financial benefit for the Spaniards since the tiny mountain farms hardly represent a living. Most of the men work in the booming building industry down by the coast. Mother's house was entirely built by men from the village and it is a really beautiful piece of work. Electo and his merry men are craftsmen within the meaning of the act.

So what do I do while I am there? I sleep, eat and read. For two days I think that this is marvellous. The next two days I think that it is marvellous, but . . . Thereafter, I long to get back to my dogs, my sheep, and my hounds. Why do we not go to the beach and swim? Have you seen a Spanish beach in summer? Have you seen what goes into the tideless Mediterranean Sea? It is fifteen years since I have swum in the Med and on that occasion, as I breasted a wave, I met a turd swimming purposefully towards me. It chased me back to the beach. I then amused myself by watching the rats playing around the broken sewage outfall pipe where it discharged its responsibility on the sand. If you want to frolic in the Med you are very welcome to all of my share of it.

I quite enjoy my visit and a dutiful son ought to visit his mother. I just wish, and I am pretty sure that Mother now wishes, that she had chosen to settle further from the Costa Blanca with its totally ghastly colony of North European expatriates. I just have a sneaking feeling that, knowing Mother, there will soon come a desire for a new house to do up and new mountains to climb. I hope she will settle somewhere that is not served by an airport graced by Charter Flights Ltd.

June sees the start of the puppy shows. I have touched on puppy walking and have suggested some of the pleasure and the pain of the selfless people concerned. Ah, I hear you say, but what's in it for them, then? Nothing for nothing, eh squire? I am truly sorry to disappoint you but there really is nothing in it for them: all they get is the puppy show.

Every hunt has a puppy show in the summer. The puppies shown are really no longer puppies; they are the ones who were out at walk the previous summer. They are now back in the kennels learning their lessons in preparation for their introduction to hunting in the autumn, when they will be about eighteen months old. The prime aim of the puppy show is to thank the puppy walkers, but it tends to be a bit of a summer binge for the hunt. In theory, it is the Master's private party, but we all know what happens to theories.

A date is decided upon after much solemn deliberation and consulting and cross-checking of diaries. This date concentrates in a wondrous manner the collective mind of the hunt staff on spring cleaning. On the day of the puppy show, thc world and its wife will see the kennels and no huntsman wants to be caught with metaphorical curlers in his hair. There will be an orgy of scrubbing, steam cleaning, polishing, whitewashing, and black bitumastic painting. The grass will be manicured, hedges clipped to the quick, weeds massacred, and the kennel boy told to get rid of his acne or risk having it painted over.

The Master will concern himself with finding judges. There are usually two judges. They are usually Very Senior Foxhunters who will add a little tone to the proceedings and raise the stock of the local mastership. There is a certain one-upmanship in being able to attract judges of note.

Puppy shows normally happen in the afternoon: three o'clock is the favourite time. Before that the Master will give a luncheon party: this is for the judges, neighbouring Masters of Hounds, visitors from afar, if the kennels is sufficiently illustrious to attract such people, local worthies, Lords of the Land (if the magisterial port be of high enough note) and any other free loader who can weasel in on the act. The rule of Reciprocity comes into play: the more people the master summons to his junketing, the more browsing and sluicing he is likely to get in return. Oh yes, the guest list can cause much agonising.

There may well be a certain predictability about the menu. There are two short-priced runners for puppy show lunches: Coronation Chicken and/or Cold Salmon. Please do not think that I am complaining, since I can confront both without a tremor and eat them with gusto, if not always very tidily; it is just that they do tend to occur pretty regularly. The one thing that is necessary is plenty of plonk. Old puppy show campaigners soon learn certain basic rules for their own comfort. Not all Masters live in palladian mansions, and even if they do, the guest list always seems to overflow whatever space may be available. This means that the luncheon will be a stand-up job. There will be a certain number of chairs and tables as there will be in most houses. The old sweat will get himself well tucked in behind the leaders to be first at the trough, even if this means a bit of bumping and boring. He will then make a determined sally and capture some of the available seating space, pausing only to tuck under the arm enough liquid rations to see him through until the pud.

These lunches are a great time to catch up on all the gossip. To find out who is doing what to whom. To fly a kite or two of your own. To start the unravelling of a reputation and to try to stop others picking holes in yours. The host's main concern will be to get the judges to the show on time, and to prevent the senior judge taking too much port on board which might just induce him to make indecent suggestions to the wife of the hunt chairman and get the afternoon off to a sticky start.

By three o'clock, the world and his wife will have assembled at the kennels. In front of the kennels, there will be a fenced-off square with a concrete pad in the middle: this is the show ring. Around this will be ranged rows of chairs, benches and straw bales for the audience, the front row being reserved for the Very Old and Bold. From the kennels there will be a chorus of excitement at all this unwonted disturbance. The hunt staff will be fussing about in very clean white kennel coats and bowler hats. The huntsman in particular will have a weather eye on one side of the ring where the benches will be entirely populated by weather-beaten men in dark suits and bowler hats. These are the visiting hunt servants who will be merciless in their appraisal of their peer and his hounds. He will also roll an eye at one of the front benches where there will be that well known trio of Col X, Lord Y and Miss Z, all masters of immense age, knowledge and seniority. They are all stone deaf and think that hounds and hunting have gone to the dogs (if you will excuse the expression). They will spend the afternoon trumpeting this fact to each other.

By now the judges should be in the ring sucking their pencils, and the proceedings get under way.

The young hounds are shown two at a time. This is because the sea of strange faces can be quite an ordeal for young hounds and they get confidence from company. Hounds are judged on conformation and movement. A hound wants to be the right shape to gallop fast and to keep on galloping for a long time; it might go a hundred miles in a single hunting day. The judges look for stamina points and pace points, all of which should be combined so as to produce a well-balanced animal that moves like quicksilver. The hounds are shown loose so that their movement can be assessed. If a hound moves right, then it follows that it must be shaped right. The kennel huntsman will have put long hours of practice into preparing the young hounds. They are tempted to stand or gallop by judiciously thrown biscuits. The judges stamp round looking stern and knowledgeable, conferring in muted voices.

Then, "Done with them, Stan."

"Thank you, sir," The couple are removed from the ring and the next couple brought in.

Poor Gaffer is appalled at all these perfectly frightful people in his yard, and goes and sits down firmly by the kennel door. Ganymede thinks it is all too, too amusing my dear. He does two circuits of the ring at top pace, then flies the fence, and lands squarely in the broad lap of old Mrs Brimblecombe. Mrs Brimblecombe disappears backwards with a consequent display of rather complicated nether garments; with her goes the bench and its entire complement of junior Brimblecombes. Wails are wailed and teeth gnashed, but in due course order, Ganymede, and the Brimblecombes are all restored to their rightful places.

The show goes on.

After all the young Doghounds have appeared, they are then brought in together and the judges start the weeding out process.

"Gaffer out," bellows the master and the unfortunate hound is carried from the ring.

"Ahhh!" says the part of the crowd that has a vested interest in Gaffer.

"Out at the elbow," says Col Y.

"Whatcher say?" screeches Miss Z.

"Clarence says the dog was out at the elbow, Mabel," bellows Lord X.

"Well, I thought he was very elbowy, whatever you say," bays Miss Z. They can keep this up all day.

One by one the puppies are removed from the ring until only three remain. The judges confer, circle, chew their pencils and nod sagely. The decision made, the Master is summoned and scribbles on his clipboard. Silence falls. The Master removes his hat and produces his well-known storm-force bellow:

"Ladies and gentlemen, the judges decision is: first Ganymede, walked by Mrs Varco." The huntsman points to Ganymede who is trying to hypnotise another biscuit out of him. "Second Captain, walked by Mrs Luscombe, and third Barker, walked by Miss Coaker."

He replaces his hat and there is a ripple of applause from the spectators.

"Nice dog that," says Col Y.

"Whatcher say?" says Miss Z.

"Clarence says . . ." but let us leave them to it.

The Bitch Hounds will be shown next and then the couples class for those who walked two puppies. The two main classes are judged straight, but the couples class can be very useful for spreading the prizes and soothing bruised egos. Wise judges take a nod and a wink from the Master.

It is tea time. As I have said, the puppy show is a day to thank the puppy walkers. In the richer hunts, they will receive a slap up tea laid on by a firm of caterers. In smaller hunts, the ladies of the hunt tend to rally round and produce a rather better tea than the caterers would, but the ladies of the hunt are bound to include the puppy walkers themselves. This never seems to worry them and I suspect that they are pleased to have the chance to show off their undoubted baking skills. If you want to sample a really first class old-fashioned tea, get yourself invited to a puppy show.

After the tea come the speeches. The Master will be anxious to get on with these as he has been watching the senior judge out of the corner of his eye. The judge has already appeared out of the huntman's house once, wiping his moustache; if he gets in there again he might well be past reclamation.

Puppy show speeches have a fixed format. The Master thanks the puppy walkers, the hunt staff, the ladies who made the tea, the world and his wife and, of course, the judges. He then calls on the judges to say a few words.

The judges thank the Master for inviting them, praise the hounds, praise the puppy walkers, and by tradition tell a story. The sort of story that judges consider fit for puppy show audiences can vary widely. Sometimes their aim is wide. On the other hand, there are certain artists who can tell a seemingly very unsuitable story and by their skill reduce even the most strait-laced of the audience to helpless laughter. The senior judge is one of these and duly performs to general acclaim. As the laughter dies down, you are almost certain to hear:

"What was he saying about the bishop, Clarence?"

That is the end of it really, and you can now collect your loved ones and go home and put your feet up in front of the telly. Unless of course you feel a touch on the elbow and there is a huntsman saying that you will just call in the house and have a drink before you go.

"I'm just popping in for a quick one, dear," you say to the wife, "and I'll be right out. Stan would be upset if I didn't go in." If the wife is young and trusting and not used to puppy shows, she might even believe you.

July

In July, there is the ritual dipping of sheep. By law every sheep in Her Majesty's realm has to be dipped twice a year. The reason for this is to zap the nasty little scab mite which can cause sheep great distress and debilitation. The process also deals with any other little passengers the sheep may be carrying, and generally freshens and tones up the system. The process involves total immersion in an evil-smelling chemical soup for the thick end of a minute. It does the sheep no end of good (always provided that they do not drown) and they hate it.

In the old days the sheep were baptised. They were lowered backwards one by one into a sunken steel tub. A man, swathed in oilskins, stood in a pit hole beside the tub and dunked each sheep manually. It was a bugger of a job, involving great physical and mental stress on all concerned. I am glad to report that things have improved. There are now slide-in and walk-in dipping systems which require less physical input manwise, and less stress on the sheep.

I have a mobile dipper. It is a large tub (holding 300 gallons) and a platform (24ft by 7½ft) on wheels. You tow it along and set it up wherever you want to dip sheep. It is a very efficient system and, at one time, I used to go contracting with it: going from farm to farm and dipping other people's sheep in the name of cashflow. It was quite a nice little earner and I used to dip something like 60,000 sheep a year and sometimes as many as 2,000 in a day. This meant that I developed the arms and shoulders of a gorilla along with the waist of a simpering maiden.

I eventually gave up contract-dipping and I will tell you for why in one word: fumes. The chemicals used in sheep dip are pretty potent and the mixture gives off fumes. The man who hangs over a seething tub of the stuff day after day may experience some discomfort. He may start to feel rather as one does when influenza is poised to strike. I did not care for this. I first consulted the manufacturer. "Ha! Ha!" they said. "What an old silly billy you are. Can't be anything to do with our dip, my dear fellow; it's marvellous stuff. Why, do you know that our chairman drinks half a pint (neat) each and every working day? Marvellous stuff. Must dash. Hope you're better soon."

I next thought of the experts of the MAFF, so I rang the Ministry. The Ministry said I wanted Health and Safety. Fine, please could I speak to them. Puff, said the Ministry, not here, you cannot. I transpired that H&S (the ungrateful bitch) had gone off with the Agricultural Training Board.

I rang the ATB.

"Ho, yus," said the ATB, "and 'oo said it was 'ere? Bloody MAFF, I suppose; cheeky old cat. Well, H&S was 'ere but it's gorn and good riddance I say: fag ends and used Kleenex all over the place. Try Weights and Measures."

I eventually discovered that Health and Safety had been wrongly filed under Incidental Increments, but it was out to lunch anyway. I got through to it about four o'clock that afternoon. It asked if I was a Notifiable Disease because if I was not then it didn't want to know me. Why did I not ring the MAFF?

After this I decided to give up contract-dipping. However, I still have my own sheep to do and I still "oblige" a few selected neighbours.

Fred and I get the dipper in position on D day-1 and get the tub filled. I reckon 0600 is a good time to start when all is fresh and cheerful. It will be a long day.

From the collecting pen, the sheep go in single file up the ramp. The theory is that as they cannot see what is in store for them, they go willingly and on the whole that is true. But is has never been true of my own sheep:

they sussed it out from the start. The lambs will run up sweetly enough, but the ewes will jib and nap and baulk: they have to be prodded up the ramp with an ever increasing level of profanity.

Even when diluted, sheep dip is nasty stuff. You do not want it on your skin, in your eyes and you neither want to swallow nor inhale it. The dipper man is festooned in protective clothing and face masks because he is going to get heavily splashed. He is also going to get very, very hot.

As each sheep gets to the top of the ramp, it teeters on the little ledge at the top of the slide. The dipper reaches across with his stick and deftly twitches a hind leg, seeing that the ewe slides backwards into the broth. There is room for maybe four ewes, or seven lambs, in the tub at the same time. It is circular so the ewes have no choice but to swim round and round whilst the dipper gets his T-shaped stick behind each head and pushes it under. Each sheep should be in the dipper for 60 seconds but some sheep, especially some lambs, would not survive the full span, and a certain amount of discretion has to be exercised. But I do not mean that the job can be skimped. The job is too important and the dip fluid too expensive for the job not to be done properly. When the time is up, a hatch is lifted and the sheep escape on to a draining platform from which they go down another ramp to freedom.

You may think that there has not been much humour so far in this chapter. But I can tell you that there is little humour to be found standing for ten hours a day swathed in pvc and face masks under a searing sun. The life of a backwoodsman is not all beer and skittles, and those who chatter about the dignity of labour tend to be those who take good care to donate their share of it to someone else. So is there no laughter? Well, of course there is: we all cried with laughter when Kenny missed his footing and slid backwards into the tub.

We all absolutely hooted when that big Suffolk tup knocked Jim arse over head and trampled him comprehensively as it lumbered back down to the pens. We are all absolutely riveted when, at bait time, the conversation turns to the real, and imagined, sexual proclivities of the inhabitants of the surrounding villages. What was meant when Mrs X displayed the OMO packet in her kitchen window? Old Man Out, of course. We make do with simple, earthy pleasures in the backwoods: you must not expect too much of us.

In the kennels, the tempo quickens somewhat in July as "Hound Exercise" begins to take the place of "Walking Out". In the old days, ponies would have appeared by the beginning of the month and the staff would array themselves in "No. 3 dress": boots, breeches, old red coat, and grey bowler hat. The pace, and the distance, of the exercise would be gradually stepped up over a two-month period so that when hunting began after the harvest, hounds would be as hard and fit as road work could get them.

Things, as they will insist on saying, are not what they used to be. These days we are cost conscious. The horses stay in the field (costing nothing) until August. We make do with the Bicycle.

The Kennel Bicycle is worthy of comment; in fact, if I were a Kipling, I would write a poem about it, especially if I could find a good Hindustani word for it (I suppose that there must be one). The Kennel Bicycle does not score very high on the social ladder. It has received little in the way of tender loving care; it has known much abuse and rough usage; it is sour, embittered, and cynical and it is ever ready to entrap the hand that adjusts the chain. It is quick and cunning too: the Kennel Bicycle, given the slightest chance, will drop its rider in the road, and then stick a handlebar where it will do the maximum damage. What the handlebar fails to achieve, the seat will finish, showing neither mercy nor compromise with certain essential parts of the anatomy. It is a treacherous machine. Halfway across a main road it will drop its chain, leaving the rider pedalling madly, but totally without effect, whilst 32 tonnes of hard-driven quarry waste bears down from the right. On the left, there may well be a maddened load of cauliflowers from Crespigny-sur-Laone. It is not a happy situation. Why then do we bother with the Kennel Bicycle? Because it's cheap, dear, because it's cheap.

It is also practical because it is possible to keep up a nice steady "hound jog" which is the natural travelling pace of a hound. It can be a maddening pace on a horse, being faster than a walk, but slower than a trot: I suppose that it would be about 4 mph. Some horses can never adapt to it, and pity the man who has to ride such an animal. The bicycle is also practical because should you wish to dismount to remove a thorn from a hound's pad, or some such, a bicycle does not suddenly take off for home with tail and stirrups flying, accompanied by half the young hounds in delirious riot. On the other hand, of course, you do not have to get off and push a horse up a hill.

Variety is the spice of hound exercise. Bugbrooke Episcopi may be an immensely picturesque village but you can get a bit sick of it when jogging through it for the thirty-ninth time. I once hunted a country that was not a very good hunting country but it was marvellous for exercise. There were miles of old chalk drove roads over the downs where you could mooch about for hours, listening to the larks and seeing only the occasional shepherd or tractor driver.

One blazing August morning we came down off the downs to the river in the valley where we stopped to give hounds a swim and a drink. The longer I looked at the gentle pellucid flow, the cooler and more inviting it looked and the hotter and sweatier I felt. A moment later I was sitting blissfully in the cooling depths, whilst hounds frolicked and gambolled about me. Another moment later and the Hunt Chairman's ancient Rover hove to on the bridge with its full complement of Chairman, Chairman's Lady, Chairman's Lady's Ancient Mother, and Chairman's Lady's Ancient Mother's Even More Ancient Spinster Sister. It was indeed fortunate that I had retained my straw hat so that I was at least able to raise it to the ladies, even if it was not really possible for me to stand up in their presence. I thought that they might want to stop and admire the hounds but they drove off rather suddenly and rather fast. The Chairman was a bit huffy about it later. I pointed out to him that the only thing visible that had not been made by God was the straw hat.

July is haymaking time. These days I have liberated myself from this particular tyranny by buying all my hay.

Whenever this remark appears in print, I get bags of letters from protesting agriculturists. I have proved conclusively that it is cheaper to buy hay than to make it. I worked it out in great detail on the back of an envelope that had contained a list of sales from the local auction mart. If I could only find that envelope I would be able to prove my point convincingly — but I suppose that if I did everybody would give up making hay and, ergo, there would be none for me to buy. It is better if I keep my secret.

People who have never done it, get a touch of the romantics about haymaking. They imagine the rhythmic swish of the scythe, sun-browned sinewy arms, earthenware jugs of cider cooling in the shade, and sweet Bessie the milkmaid coming along for the rustic equivalent of a bit of Whey hey hey! Heaven preserve your innocence, my children: haymaking is a bore.

I well remember getting a letter from an earnest reader taking me to task after I had written a blistering exposé of making hay. He told me how I should do it and of course he was quite right except that his method involved the use of at least four tractors and six men. All I ever had was myself and Igor. Igor was a battered Czechoslovakian tractor. To prevent everybody writing to the publishers and excoriating me for not buying British, I bought Igor because he was cheap, and because he was there. The Czechos actually build good solid no-nonsense tractors. They also put good roomy cabs on their tractors with room for a passenger, two collies and a bait bag. British tractors (and most of them are not, anyway) are very parsimonious about the cab.

Haymaking is quite simple. You cut the grass; leave it to bake in the sun for a week; turn it to get it thoroughly dry; then you bale it and bear it triumphantly to the barn. If you can guarantee ten consecutive days of sun and breeze, it is a doddle. Who amongst you would like to make such a guarantee in England?

Modern efficient mowers can be fixed to the tractor in about five minutes. My mower was second-hand and profoundly embittered. It used to take me half a day, much assorted swearing, and many mashed knuckles to hitch it on to Igor. As soon as I started up, there would be some dreadful metallic screeching.

The Mechanic cometh. Farm mechanics are dour young men covered in oil and acne. The two things that they are really good at is sucking their teeth in an offensive manner and charging you fifteen quid an hour (or part thereof). True to form, their first reaction on seeing my mower would be to suck their teeth. They would then tap the machine with a multi-purpose reciprocating ratchet and launch into a variation of the "Didn't — know — there — were — any — of — these — still — about — and — you — can't — get — spares — for — them — no — more — mate" theme. I do not know what the incidence of bodily assaults on farm mechanics may be, but I should not be surprised if the figure is high.

There is a certain satisfaction in mowing: watching the thick green shear of grass tumbling behind the mower, whilst the rectangle of standing grass gets smaller and smaller. I quite enjoy tractor driving in small doses, especially on a fine day when you can take the doors off the tractor, light the pipe and get Radio 4 on the wireless. Igor had a wireless. One day, the soaking wet senior collie lay on it; then Igor no longer had a working wireless. Never mind, I used to sing instead.

We all know about the smell of hay cooking in the sun. It is very satisfying to walk across the nicely baking rows. It is not so satisfying to see it sogging in the rain. I once sold a field of mowing-grass to two brothers. They cut it. For two weeks the sun blazed down on it and they never came near it. On the fifteenth day they came to turn it and the monsoon arrived. It rained solidly for about three weeks. Every day I would go through the hay field on my way to look at the sheep. Every day one of the brothers would be standing in the field, leaning on a prong (pitch fork) with the rain dripping off his hat brim. Every day, whichever brother was on duty would say exactly the same thing: "By, it's slow to make." They never did make it. It turned black where it lay and we pushed it into the quarry with a buck rake.

When one turns the hay, there are several different machines for the job: turners, wufflers, pheasants. I had a thing called a Hay Bob which is Dutch and very efficient. You whizz round the field scattering the hay abroad so that the sun gets to all the bits and "kills" it. Then you whizz round again putting it in nice fluffy "windrows" so that the wind can get through it. Next it rains for two days. You go back six squares and miss a turn. Then you start all over again.

The time will probably come when the hay is fit to bale. Balers are beyond my mechanical understanding so I used to get a contractor to come and do it.

Contractual Sods Law dictated that the contractor was never ready when the hay was. CSL goes on to state "that the party of the second part hereinafter

referred to as the Contractor shall upon arrival immediately commence to tell the party of the first part hereinafter referred to as the Payer intimate and salacious
details of his latest marital infidelity notwithstanding the
fact that he is physically totally hideous and has terminal
halitosis. On commencing the job hereinafter referred to
as the Work the contractor shall do two rounds of the
field thereinafter he shall spend two hours upended in
the gizzard of the baler using totally regrettable
language. On the recommencement of the work it shall
immediately start to piss down with rain hereinafter
referred to as ★★★★★★★" and so on and so forth even
unto insanity and bedlam.

In the old days, all the bales were little cubes weighing about 50lbs. These had to be loaded onto a trailer,
carried to the barn and elevated up onto the stack. The
elevator is a continuous belt and so is working with it.
As the stack gets higher and higher, it will self-evidently
get nearer the roof. Anyone who has stacked bales
under a corrugated iron roof on which the July sun is
beating down will understand how a *true* agricultural
thirst is created.

Stacking bales is not a lovesome job. In later years, I
made big bales. These are big cylinders weighing
between 300 and 400lbs. You do not hoy them about
by hand; you have a hydraulic loader on the front of the
tractor with two vicious looking hydraulic jaws which
clamp the bale. You do the whole operation from the
seat of the tractor. As my friend Sid says, "If you can't
do the job from the tractor and it is too heavy for the
wife to do, then it is not worth doing."

It is possible that by now you have some idea as to why

I gave up making hay. I no longer have expensive machinery sitting about sulking for fifty weeks of the year. Bad hay you make yourself you are then stuck with. Bad hay sent by the merchant gets sent back with a bollocking. I rest my case.

July sees one of the great festivals of the hunting year: Peterborough Hound Show. It would be wrong to describe Peterborough as the Crufts of the hound world: the other way about would be better. It would be equally wrong to say that Peterborough is part of the East of England Show. However, one cannot but notice that some sort of agricultural show does take place on the periphery of the hound show and, frankly, greatly adds to the inconvenience.

There are five other major hound shows: at Ardingly (south), Honiton (west), Builth Wells (Wales and Border counties), Harrogate (north), and Rydal (Lakeland).

The theory behind hound shows is that they give people a chance to see hounds other than the ones they see in their own kennels and that this stops them thinking that their own geese are really swans. The very real danger is that people get too keen on showing and pothunting. Old and influential masters might (just might) start to get more pleasure out of receiving a nice silver trophy on a nice warm summer day than they would out of tickling up their rheumatism on a freezing January hillside. This might (just might) make them think twice about using as a stallion hound Gaffer who is plain but a 22-carat worker, when they might (just might) use the beautiful Galliard who is as soft as shit but might (just might) get some show winners. Such things have been known to happen. There was a hound who won a lot in the fifties and was in great demand as a stallion hound. It was subsequently revealed (there are no secrets in hunting) that this beautiful dog was never allowed to go hunting in case he should get a blemish.

A friend of mine went to look at some hounds in Wales. In one lodge of the kennel there were tired muddy hounds who obviously had had a hard hunt the day before. The hounds in the other lodge were sleek and shiny. Why so? wondered my friend. His hosts chuckled at his saxon innocence: the first lot were the hunting hounds and the others were the show hounds, there's simple, isn't it? There's bloody dishonest too.

Hound shows are fine as long as they are regarded as a jolly day out amongst one's chums.

Peterborough has come to be regarded as the major hound show, mainly because it takes place in the Midlands which used to be the fashionable heart of hunting. There is little good hunting in the Midlands these days, but there is much fashion.

At the lesser shows, you may well see Masters in shirt sleeves and even cloth caps. This would never do at Peterborough: Peterborough requires dark suits and highly polished shoes. Up to ten years ago you wouldn't have dreamed of going there without bowler hat, rolled umbrella and stiff collar. However, the brave Master who first went to the show in a soft collar deserves a medal: I remember that it caused quite a stir at the time. They are the norm now. ("You cannot get a stiff collar starched properly these days, old boy." Rhubarb.) The bowler hat is presently in decline, which is sad in its way, but they are rather a nuisance. The umbrella remains strong because there is nearly always a thunderstorm at Peterborough.

What do the ladies wear? How should I know about that sort of thing? Well, if you really insist, you will have to hang on for a moment whilst I ask Control. Right, well, the answer is whatever you would wear for a garden party — but I regret to report she has given up wearing a hat (disgraceful).

Right, provided that you are properly dressed and promise not to embarrass me, perhaps you would like to troll along with me to the show. Just this once we will avoid the obligatory two-hour traffic jam on the A1 and assume that we have completed the yomp from the Red Car Park where we vice-presidents get tucked away. The hound show has its own little enclosure in the middle of the show ground, surrounded by menacing multi-widgeted combine harvesters and hot dog stalls. It has its own browsing and sluicing arrangements and its own loos; for which relief you will be truly thankful. The actual show ring sits in the middle of the enclosure with the sutlers' tents at one end and the kennels at the other.

Once inside, there are instant splashes of colour. The hunt servants who are showing hounds do so in full hunting fig (except spurs): there will be a milling crowd of red, green and the odd yellow coat, whiter than white breeches and gleaming boots.

"Hello, Peter."

"Hullo, sir: how are you?" Peter does a sweep with his hunting cap. Hunt servants are one of the last repositories of good manners left in the realm. Peter worked for me when he was a boy (and I not much older). He is now an up-and-coming huntsman and I a departing one.

"You're looking well."

"You're looking fit too, sir. May be carrying a bit too much fettle. Time you got the bike out." Peter used to dine out on my velocipedic ineptitude. One day I rode my bike into a ditch and bent it. He was laughing so much that he did not see me nick his bike and slip away with the hounds. A five-mile hike home with a broken bicycle does wonders for the sense of humour.

One of the great pleasures of Peterborough is that you find gathered there foxhunters from all over the realm whom one would seldom otherwise see. There is a chance to talk over times past, to freshen old friend-ships, and to sharpen old rivalries. There is also a chance to catch up on the gossip. The talk is all about hounds, hunting and, it has to be said, adultery. I do not suppose that foxhunters are any more adulterous than stockbrokers or, for all I know, local government officials. But maybe they are: after all, a lot of adrenalin gets stimulated out hunting and the MFH is one of the few remaining examples of naked power (if you will pardon the expression). That is the theory, at least. One of the reasons I became an MFH is because I thought that it would automatically entitle me to unlimited nooky. I am here to tell you that that side of the business was pretty much a flop (if you will pardon the expression) as far as I was concerned.

The excuse for this fest is the hound show, so we had better have a look at that.

The show ring is a covered rectangle with tiers of seats on all sides. For years, my seat has been in the front row of the North stand. When I was very young, I came in at the end of the row. At the end of the row, the eyes are clear and the torsos trim. As the grim reaper empties seats, I am creeping nearer and nearer the middle of the row. This indicates seniority. The nearer the middle, the higher the incidence of decaying chests collapsing into burgeoning bellies and once firm jaws becoming bejowled. The middle of the row is all liver spots, shaking hands, and general structural decay.

Opposite me, across the ring, is the "Cabinet Bench" where all the real nobs sit. The prizes are likely to go somewhere along this bench. The study of consternation and whitening knuckles on the benches opposite should the judging go awry is entertainment in itself.

The Doghounds are judged in the morning and the Bitch Hounds after luncheon. There are classes for single hounds, couples, and two couples. Each pack brings in its entry separately. The hound is loosed and the huntsman persuades it to run up and down the ring by chucking biscuits. You may think that this sounds easy, but showing hounds well is an art. Hounds are judged on movement and conformation, but we learnt about that at the puppy show I think.

I am not a dedicated watcher of showing and after a couple of classes I feel an overwhelming need for a gin and tonic to see me through the rest of the morning. It is a guinea to a gooseberry that I shall find many like-minded brethren in the drink tent. I always go back to watch the Stallion Hound class which is worth watching. Then it is time for luncheon.

The luncheon at Peterborough has been through some purple patches including a merry burst of salmonella one year, with vice presidents laying out their kit all over the place, and being carted away by the van load. I missed that year.

The luncheon was also the scene of one of my greatest coups.

Do you remember the Black Bomber case? Let me refresh your memory. A certain man went to Glasgow on business. In the evening he met a lady of joy. They found their conversation so mutually satisfying that they decided to continue it in his room. It was there that a physical problem obtruded, or, to be more accurate, refused to. The lady then produced two black capsules which she thought might raise the tone of the proceedings. The capsules did indeed have a marked effect to the extent that the lady's undoubted conversational powers failed her and she felt compelled to do a runner. The punter's flow of soul was by no means diminished and he felt an urgent desire for more company, to the extent that he ran naked, screaming and rampant through the corridors of the hotel demanding conversation. It took six of Glasgow's finest to suppress his urges and, having covered his conversation piece with a helmet, to cart him off to the slammer.

It was hardly surprising that this incident, which had happened shortly before, became something of a talking point at the Peterborough luncheon, the masters taking a keen interest in matters libidinous. There was a certain amount of jocular cut and thrust about the "Black Bombers", and a bit on the lines of: "But just as a matter of interest, Old Boy, I wonder how one gets the things. Not a word to Daphne, mind." (If you knew Daphne, you would understand his concern.)

Now it just so happened that on my way through the agricultural show that morning, I had paused at a stall selling animal health products and had purchased a tin of Orfoids.

Orf, or to give it its snappier demotic title "Contagious Pustular Dermatitis" is a nasty skin disease to which young lambs are particularly prone. Orfoids cure it. Orfoids seem to contain sulphur, Stockholm Tar, and goodness knows what else. They are black shiny pastilles.

I pulled the tin from my pocket and put an Orfoid on the table. There was a respectful silence as all eyes focused on the pill.

"I don't suppose you could spare one, or two," said someone tentatively.

"Two quid a piece," I said. The contents of the tin were sold in a flash.

After a return trip to the animal health product stall to replace my tin, I spent the next hour leaning non-chalantly against the screen outside the gents' loo which was more than usually busy. I missed two classes of the bitch judging, so brisk was the business. I have never yet had any complaints from any of my customers that day, so I can only assume that the Orfoids did whatever it was that was expected of them. Daphne certainly looked very cheerful when last I saw her.

August

I suppose that with the coming of August you will all be chucking the buckets and spades and the Wife's Mother in the back of the car. You will then rush off lemming-like to sit in the traffic jams which are the nearest most of you will get to the seaside.

I will tell you a sad story about traffic jams. For a short while I lived in Somerset, north of Taunton. For one summer, the embryonic M5 motorway came to a shuddering halt at the end of my road, and three lanes of traffic had to filter onto the old A38 which used to seize up if two horse-drawn carts met each other. Every summer Saturday there would be three lines of stationary west-bound traffic shimmering and sweltering in the sun for hours on end. The sad story is of the Londoner who had sat for six hours awaiting his turn to get from the M5 jam to the A38 jam. When he finally got to the junction, he asked the policeman how much farther it was to Liverpool.

The sensible Backwoodsman tries to avoid all form of travel in August. The exception to this might be if he is going north to shoot at the grouse of (and be fleeced at poker by) dear old Buffy.

I do not shoot grouse myself; in fact I have very little to do with them because I find the wretched things totally inedible. I was once presented with grouse at a luncheon. My first stab with the fork bent the said utensil. I was given a new and apparently reinforced fork, and I stabbed the bird again with some vigour. This time it took off like an exocet, whizzed past my host's left ear, badly damaged an ancestor on the wall and bounced to the floor where it was fielded and brought back to me by an obliging labrador. I have never been enthusiastic about eating grouse since.

That is quite enough about grouse. I am not quite sure how we got on to the wretched things anyway. Oh yes, we were discussing the lack of mobility amongst Backwoodsmen in August. The sensible Backwoodsman will pull up his drawbridge (if he has one) and stay at home. Should his family agitate for sea and sand, let him send them to a boarding house in Clacton, by chara-banc, then let him put his feet up with a sigh, light a cigar, and soak up the peace and quiet.

In this part of the Backwoods, August is the month for shows. There is a local show every Saturday. They follow each other in immutable succession and to a time-honoured pattern.

There will be two marquees larger than the rest (they move from show to show each week) and the Secretary's caravan and the ladies' loo which also follow the drum.

One marquee houses the produce section. Here will be monstrous radishes; tumescent marrows which, if pricked, might well take the whole tent and half the village with them; spring onions of stupendous tuberosity; and of course the leeks.

Leeks in the north of England are not just vegetables to eat, they are a way of life. They are grown to an enormous size. They are coddled, flattered and prayed to by their keepers. They are fed on amazing mixtures of great antiquity and complexity (blood comes into nearly all of them), the secret of which is passed down through families. No formula for a secret rocket fuel is more closely guarded.

The security for the leeks themselves is just as tight. Passions run high amongst the leek men. There are dark tales of skulduggery, leek napping, and bombing with weed killer. Leek men tend to be also keepers of Alsatians and Dobermanns. That tumbledown shed at the bottom of the garden that you dismissed as probably being the outside khazi (netty in these parts) probably has more sensitive listening equipment than GCHQ and a General-Purpose Machine Gun to boot.

I was once presented with a second-prize leek. It filled the whole larder and took a week to eat.

It tasted of Leek.

The marquee is not made for vegetables alone. There will be cakes (be sure to buy one afterwards), buns, scones, flower arrangements, childrens' handicrafts; and there will be Dressed Sticks.

The craft of stick dressing is an ancient one. The traditional shepherd's stick has a hazel shank and a 'horn heid' crook made from tup's horn. You can either have a neck crook where the hook is big enough to catch a sheep by the neck; or a leg crook where the crook is shaped to catch a sheep just above the hock. The long winter evenings in front of the fire were the traditional time for making sticks. Many men were very skilled at the job and produced beautiful carvings in the horn. The skill still thrives and the main artists are still the hill shepherds. They would not be human if they did not want to display their craft and so every show has a dressed stick section. There are usually classes for ornamental sticks, shepherds' sticks, and walking sticks.

The ornamental sticks are just that, carved in fantastic shapes. Here is a fox running over the curve of the horn with three hounds in hot pursuit. There is a mouse eating a piece of cheese at the end of the horn, whilst a large tabby cat stalks over the curve. There are kingfishers, collie dogs, sheep, intricately entwined foliage, all carved out of the solid horn, with minute detail and infinite patience.

The working and walking sticks are plain and functional but no less beautiful in their simplicity. A "horn heid" stick quickly becomes an old friend; warm and friendly in the hand. It becomes an extension of the arm, a support, a brake on a steep hillside, a companion. You will very likely have more than one and choose the stick that suits your mood of the moment, or the one that is best adapted to the work in hand. Then there will be the "mart" stick, the high days' and holidays' stick which you wear when you are out on the skite. Because that is what you do; you *wear* a stick, and you would no more think of going out without one than you would think of leaving your trousers behind.

Sometimes I am the Dressed Stick Steward at our local show. These sticks are made for walking and sometimes members of the great British public put too liberal an interpretation on this fact — but not whilst I am Dressed Stick Steward they do not; not unless they want to start walking with one.

I suppose that whilst I have been wittering on, you have all been waiting in suppressed excitement, dying to know what happens in the other marquee? Booze, of course, gallons of it.

Outside the marquees there is always a show of sheep. There will always be a sheep dog trial, but do not expect quite the polish of the version you see on the telly. There will be a dog show, a gymkhana, a fancy dress parade, stalls and side shows; a bouncing castle, tossing the straw bale, a pillow-fight on the greasy pole, Cumbrian wrestling, a tug of war, and sometimes, heaven help me, a Parade of Hounds, which really deserves a section to itself.

All through the afternoon, the local silver band will be thumping away, alternating with the local pipe band. As the noise of the music increases — so will the level of noise and consumption in the booze tent be rising. By mid afternoon, they will be four deep at the bar and there will be macho displays of tent pole climbing. I was no mean exponent of this slightly esoteric art in my younger days, but gave it up after a slightly unfortunate accident. I had climbed to the top of the pole (tumultuous applause) and there my trousers got firmly hanked in the contraption that kept the canvas up. I eventually came down, but most of my trousers sulked and refused to follow. I decided that my pole-climbing activities had come to an end.

Sometimes I am Sheep Steward. This requires no more skill than being able to write 1–2–3 on a piece of paper and having pockets large enough to carry the rosettes and the envelopes with the prize money. Most of those showing sheep will be shepherds. The sheep may be their employer's or their own "pack sheep" (sheep belonging to the shepherd but which run with the main flock as part of the shepherd's perks: pack sheep have never been known to ail, they are always lamb twins, and never, ever die).

There will be a class for ewes, gimmers (ovine virgins trembling on the brink of matrimony), ewe lambs and tup lambs. The judge will be some prominent local (but not too local) sheep man.

Each pen is "loused" into the ring and the judge looks at them sideways, backwards, front ways. The judge will give a sheep a sharp double tap with his stick which is a sign for the proud owner to catch it up and hold it: it has been "pulled in" for the final line-up. When all the sheep are captured and lined up, the judge will submit them to a minute personal inspection: fleece, eyes, teeth, et al. Competitors may be moved up, or down, the row. At last the judge will prod the steward who is smoking his pipe in a corner of the ring and dreaming about whatever it is that Sheep Stewards dream about when they should be concentrating on what is going on, urging him to say simply, "From the top" — that is, distribute the rosettes from the top of the line.

I have mentioned the business of parading hounds at a show. I write about it only with reluctance, such is the hatred that I bear for this wretched business. You might not think that it would promote such strong feelings: after all, it is only a matter of trotting round the ring with the hounds; then galloping round a couple of times, blowing the horn and finally stopping in the middle to take your hat off to the Show President.

I could tell you that the reason for my dislike is because a parade entails a lot of extra work and some extra expense. It entails dressing up like Father Christmas on what is certain to be the only hot day of the summer. A parade is certainly trying on the nerves. One wretched huntsman waiting in the collecting ring found that the event in front of him was a mock battle enacted by the Royal Marines: it took two days to collect all the hounds.

A hound parade was the scene of one of the earliest of the many humiliations that have scattered my career as a huntsman and that is why I hate them. Just for you, I will pick the scab on a wound that has never really healed.

It was my first summer as an MFH and my first parade of hounds. The showground was in an idyllic setting overlooking the English Channel which was deep blue in the hot August sunshine. I was in no mood to enjoy the view. My new boots were pinching and my raw nerve ends were made worse by the fact that the show was maintaining a stately progress two hours behind schedule.

My hour came at last. Pouring with sweat and gibbering with nerves, I steered my horse into the ring which was surrounded by a blur of expectant faces. The ring was set up for the show jumping which would follow on later.

There was a water jump.

All the hounds rushed across the arena to lie panting in the water jump.

What is supposed to happen in a parade is that the huntsman gallops round the ring, tootling his horn in a jolly fashion, whilst his happy hounds frolic and gambol around him, and the merry crowd holloa and applaud.

What happened in this case was that the hounds steadfastly (and very sensibly) refused to leave the cooling depths and shade of the water jump. I was eventually reduced to trailing disconsolately around the periphery of the ring making sad wailings on my horn. My whipper-in followed politely fifteen yards behind, the space that should have contained the pack being null and void.

I eventually persuaded my hounds to follow me out of the ring and back to the lorry park. If you thought that my cup of bitterness was carrying a good head of froth then you would be absolutely right. But even then Fate was hefting the knuckleduster in the pocket.

The lorry park was in a far corner of the vast field that held the show. Amongst all the lorries and through all the comings and goings of a busy day a hare had been lying up.

She jumped up in the middle of the pack.

My horse, overcome by the sudden excitement, bucked me off.

The whole caboodle went straight through the middle of the main ring in full cry, causing grief and unhappiness amongst the Childrens' Mounted Fancy Dress. Miniature cowboys and Queen Elizabeths were scattered to the four winds and the Red Shadow lay bawling in the water jump.

Hare and hounds were out of the other side of the ring and going well: straight to the cliffs where, in thickets of blackthorn, furze and brambles innumerable foxes waited to take their part in the entertainment.

It was 9 o'clock that night when I finally staggered into my little bungalow and collapsed into a chair, weary and miserable beyond belief.

There came a knock on the door. What now? It was my kennel huntsman. He asked politely if he could take charge of the humane killer for the night; "just in case like". He was a wise man.

Now perhaps you understand why it is that I do not like parading hounds.

So what else happens in August that is worthy of note? Well, of course, we start hunting. I like to start by the tenth of August, just to show the shooters that they cannot have all the fun and because I like an early start.

In most hunting countries, it is not possible to start hunting until the harvest is finished. We are fortunate in Northumberland in having miles of hill country where grain only appears in cornflake packets or bottles (not necessarily in that order) and there is really nothing to stop the start.

The August meets are deep in the back of the hills. This is some of the wildest country in England. To put the area in perspective allow me to lay some statistics on you. There are twenty miles of hill through which there is no road. The hills rise to 2,500 feet. It is a land of peat hag, moss and heather; of crag and rock clitter; of wind-blasted bent grass and stunted thorn. It is the home of the curlew and the raven and the hardy black-faced sheep. The people who live and work here are, perforce, hardy too; most of them bred to the life through many generations. They live in isolated steadings struggling for shelter in lonely valleys with names like Bleakhope, Sourhope, and Starveall. Even in these softer days, the lives of these people are hard and physically demanding. Jock's shepherding round entails ten miles' walking — twice a day. In the winter the steadings may be cut off for days, or even weeks, at a time. Life in the hills is no soft option.

I usually fix the first meet at Gilbert's place. Gilbert and his two sons, Jock and Jamie, farm some two thousand acres on the edge of the known world. His front drive is four careful, low gear, miles long.

We meet at first light to get the benefit of the cool of the morning; not that August runs to much in the way of heat these days.

The alarm goes off at half past three. I pride myself at being good at getting up in the morning, but I do not think that anyone is really at their best at the ungodly hour of half past three. I stagger about putting on the kettle, shaving, struggling to get both legs down one leg of the plus fours. The first cup of tea starts the system going. I fill the thermos and pack the sandwiches in the oilskin bag.

Jessica is my personal Patterdale terrier. She is a little coal-black scrap of muscle and whipcord, with a temper like a chain saw. She knows exactly what early morning bags and tackety boots betoken, and she will sit quivering beside the bag, terrified lest she be left behind.

Rupert the ATV is already on the trailer, which is on the pickup, which is in the shed. It is still pitch dark as Jess and I walk across the yard. As we bump down the farm track, there is only one set of car lights on the main road below: they turn up the valley so I know there is at least one other keen sportsman about.

The road follows the river up what must be one of the most beautiful valleys in the country. Darkness is beginning to pale as I creep cautiously up the twisty road. The previous car has cleared the sheep who like to lie on the tarmac at night, but they have returned and stand blinking sleepily in the head lights until a blast of the horn scatters them.

By the time I turn off onto Edwin's road the great hills are looming up in the grey dawn light. For about a mile, the road runs along a precipice: as they would say in the Navy, "Nothing to port; nothing to starboard" — it is a long way down to the burn should the concentration wander.

There are some half dozen people at the meet; some on foot and a few shepherds with their bikes. It is not horse country up here: some of the peat hags would swallow a horse.

There is an air of suppressed excitement as the hounds come tumbling out of the lorry. It matters not how often a person hunts, nor how many years they do it for, the magic of the first morning of new season always comes with pristine freshness.

There is a pristine freshness for the midges up here too. With whoops of delight they home in on a bit of fresh flesh; they are the size of a pheasant and wear clogs. However, I have some very good stuff called Repel 100 which keeps them at bay even from my succulence.

The huntsman, Stan, strikes off across the steep fell-side with effortless stride. Hounds fan out on the hill and disappear into the huge bracken bed, reappearing occasionally as flashes of white amongst the dark green. Now it is easy to see why hill huntsmen favour light-coloured hounds: they are easily seen on distant hillsides.

Some hounds appear on a piece of bare ground, high on the face: they are moving in single file, heads down and sterns lashing: "feathering". They have touched on the overnight drag of a fox.

From the deep brackens below them comes a high-pitched whimper.

The highout hounds hesitate.

From the bracken bed comes old Pagan's deep-throated roar: "Fox! Fox!" he bellows. The others fly to that well-known note and there is a crash of music as the whole pack joins in.

I am on the track in the valley bottom, and I stop the ATV. Jess stands quivering on the petrol tank, ears pricked.

There are occasional glimpses of hounds amongst the thick growth, but most of the progress has to be followed by ear: the wild, wonderful, thrilling sound of a pack of hounds in full cry. Even after more than forty years, it still makes my back hairs tingle.

We can see Stan's head and shoulders sticking out of the bracken; his occasional musical cheer adds to the excitement.

Hounds have divided. They now sound to be in three lots. We are obviously into a litter of cubs.

A shout; Jock is pointing. A lithe brown shape slips out of the top of the bracken and is away over the hill top. Within a minute three couple of hounds come out of the bracken, chiming away on the line. Jamie is on the hilltop. He strides away in their wake.

There is a swelling cry in the bracken bed. A fox appears across a bit of bare ground, then hounds. The main body seems to be together now. The cry surges up and down the hill. The fox is turning short. The cry stops suddenly. There is a quivering in the brackens and that unmistakable low growling. Stan comes tumbling down the steep face to where a swirling mass of hounds are beating down the growth.

"Who-whoop," he yells. At least that is the conventional way of reproducing the noise in print. The first fox of a new season.

From the other end of the bracken bed comes a long drawn-out holloa. The remainder of the pack have been hunting steadily at that end and now we see them straining away towards the skyline. Stan cheers his lot on to their cry.

It is time to gain a bit of height. The walkers are moving steadily up the brae with the apparent effortlessness of long practice. Now, if I nip along to the end of the bracken bed, there is a nice bit of bare hillside, steep, but negotiable. I drop into low gear, stand up on the pedals to keep my weight forward, and the ATV cheerfully grinds its way up the five hundred feet to the crest.

What a view: a great sweeping bowl of heather and peat hag with hills rolling away beyond; green, brown and purple with flowering heather, and cloud shadows racing across them. Those far hills must be forty or fifty miles away. However, this is no time for day dreaming. Every view is improved if it contains a pack of hounds and, at the moment, this one does not.

I get the binoculars out and glass the surround. Nothing. No, wait a bit, the sheep are just starting to "scar" (run up together) on the opposite hill, and there hounds are, a rapidly moving mass of white dots, "coming in" towards us; that is a relief.

I start the engine and Jess jumps up in front of me. It is bump and jar now over the "bull snouts" (grass tussocks), a horribly uncomfortable journey. Through a peat hag where old diggings give me considerable problems, creep down one side, sog through the slime in the bottom, and hope that the four-wheel drive will claw me out the other side without "cowping" (turning upside down). I want to get to the top of that "knowe" or rounded hill in front of me to get a better view.

Hounds are spread out like a flock of gulls on the far hill, hunting steadily across and up the slope. I know where that fox is headed. Over the top of the hill lie several thousand acres of sitka spruce and a multiple fox situation.

Twenty minutes later, I have ground across the valley and bumped, jolted, and scrabbled my way to the top of Herd's Law (2,300 feet). The sun is already warm on the back. However much I want to get on, the view makes me pause. To the east the hills roll down to the patchwork fields of the in-bye ground and on to the sea, showing blue in the fine weather. On the other side, mile upon mile of rolling hills disappear into the blue distance.

Immediately below me lies the green carpet of the forest, thrown over a series of precipitous hills. This remote place is a great vulpine reservoir. The cry comes floating up as little parties of hounds go rejoicing after different foxes. There are probably enough for one apiece. We shall spend many long days in these trees through the winter and hounds will catch many foxes there that we shall never know about.

The CB radio crackles: "Big Daddy, Big Daddy (well what else should I be known as?), do you copy?"

"Aye, roger."

"This is Ragman. Where are they about?" I tell him and his reply is most regrettable bearing in mind the fact that you are not supposed to use words like that on channel. Anyway, the upshot is that Ragman reckons he is going home. What of Big Daddy? What shall he do?

There is only one thing to do. Jess and I settle ourselves down in the sun. I settle my back comfortably against Rupert's rear wheel, unpack the sandwiches and flask, and listen to the music of hounds echoing up from the deep valleys below.

I suppose you might think that that is quite enough about hunting for one month? Well, just hang about; life is not as simple as all that and I really cannot let August pass without telling you about the Boot Hounds.

This is a flashback, you understand, but that is an approved, nay applauded, trick of the cinematographic trade and I naturally have half an eye on Hollywood and the sale of the film rights of this book. You may think that there is not enough sex and violence, but I am sure that a good director can sort out little problems like that and Miss Streep and I can work on the additional material.

Many years ago I was hunting a little pack of hounds in the south of England. One fine August morning the Boot Hounds landed on my doorstep.

There were four of them. Three were variations on a Bloodhound × Foxhound theme and only old Thunder was pure Bloodhound. How and why were they there?

Once upon a time there was an old lady who lived in a forest and kept a little pack of buckhounds to hunt the fallow deer. The forest and the buck belong to the old lady's brother. The course of family relationships does not always run smoothly and there came a falling out betwixt brother and sister, the cause of which I know not and it is none of our business anyway. Whatever the cause, the brother reared up like a piece of fried bread and told the sister to take herself and her hounds off and never to darken his forest again.

The old lady was made of stern stuff, however, and if she could not hunt one thing then she was jolly well going to hunt another, so she became a huntress of men. No, no, not like that; really, your minds work in quite a disgraceful way. She hunted what is technically known as the "Clean Boot". I do not want to be too technical, but what happens is that you have a man who runs. He is given whatever "law" is considered sufficient. The hounds are presented with some item of the quarry's clothing and they then follow his scent. The best hounds for this job are bloodhounds but they tend to wallow in the scent a bit and if you want to sharpen things up, you might bring in some foxhound blood; it gives a bit of drive and oomph to the proceedings. That is roughly what it is all about.

Our old lady clean booted very happily for a while, that is until she fell on her head (off her horse) which is definitely not a recommended procedure. The hounds were disbanded. Through a chain of coincidences and chances, which I will not bore you with, I found the Famous Four sitting demurely on my doorstep one morning all neatly parcelled up with blue ribbon.

I had a vague sort of idea that it might be quite fun to hunt the Clean Boot when I was not hunting foxes. I thought there might be some good sport to be had. And, to a certain extent, I was right.

The Boot Hounds had only been in the kennels a few days when I received an SOS. There had been a major "coming-out" dance in the neighbourhood and a friend of mine had been called upon to billet some of the visiting poodlefakers over the weekend. He was having a hard time of it.

"Right load of wilters, old boy. Blighters spend all the time draped over my chairs with all the windows shut. Pasty-faced shower of poofters. They need a bit of fresh air and exercise. Bring the Boot Hounds over on Saturday evening and we'll give the buggers a good rousting."

I have to admit to a certain reluctance. My brief acquaintance with the Boot Hounds suggested that good order and discipline were not high on their list of priorities and I really wanted a little more time to bring them into the paths of righteousness. However, here was a friend in trouble and the Code of the Backwoodsman demanded that I ride to the rescue.

Behind the friend's farm were a thousand acres of virgin

downland, covered in rough grass and gorse bushes: a haunt of picnickers and nicknickers and ideal for a bit of clean booting.

Word spread about the proposed jolly and a crowd of people gathered to have a look, including a largish mounted contingent. I was distressed to note that these included Big X and Arrogant Y. X+Y was an equation that usually equalled tears for somebody.

After knocking the dust off several large ones, I began to feel more confident. We had persuaded some youth who ran for Oxford that he needed to keep himself fit — anyway, he fancied himself quite a bit. We set him off, keeping back a pair of his socks, and then we had a few more confidence-building lotions.

The confidence was shaken somewhat when we let the Boot Hounds out of the trailer. They set off with a great cry and started vigorously hunting a £50,000 brood mare round her paddock.

Order was restored. The somewhat chastened Boot Hounds were shown the socks and immediately went wild with enthusiasm, which just goes to show that different things affect different people in different ways. The Wilters were driven protesting limply into the backs of Land Rovers; after all, this was all for their benefit and they were going to enjoy it whether they liked it or not. And at last we set off.

I must say that the four Boot Hounds did have a tremendous cry for such a small pack. The evening was warm and sunny and scent was poor but they revelled in every yard of it, booming and bellowing with pleasure. Poor old Thunder, advanced age required her to sit down and rest every hundred yards, but even then she continued to raise her jowls to Heaven and proclaim her happiness.

It was all really rather good fun. The Boot Hounds howled and boomed. I tootled my horn and cheered them on, my cheers being echoed by Big X and Arrogant Y who had taken to the host's hospitality in a serious way. A glance back showed the Land Rovers bumping along on the hill with at least one bright young thing relieving himself of the excesses of last night whilst hanging out of the back.

Problems arose.

I have already mentioned that the down was a favourite resort of picnickers and those interested in intensive nature study. A fine August Saturday is liable to bring large numbers of such groups out to play. Our runner took a perverse pleasure in setting a course as close to as many of these as was possible.

Imagine, I beg of you, that you are one of a blameless family party. You have set out in a spirit of goodwill and the family car. Such is the extent of your goodwill on such a lovely day that you have brought the wife's mother along, in spite of the fact that the old bat has never ceased to moan and complain from the moment you finally got her stuffed into the back seat.

Anyway, there you are, all settled down on the tartan rug, the tranny nicely turned up to drown Gran's whingeing; one child crying and one sulking which is really a pretty good average — good enough to rate the outing a success so far. The fish-paste sandwiches are going down a treat, too. You have just belched happily and Mum has said, "Manners, Dad!", when a great sweaty runner goes thundering by.

"Ooooo! Look," you all say. "A bloke running, well I never."

A sound grows, even impinging on the best that Radio One can provide "OWWWWW! OWWWWW!" (might almost be Radio One, come to think of it).

It grows louder.

Suddenly they are upon you: huge, black dogs, big as bulls (you tell Wilf later), howling and snuffling and wuffling and drooling. The fish-paste sandwiches are gone with two great gulps of Growler's jowls. Caesar places two massive paws on Gran's bosom, knocks her bustle over apex out of her folding chair and comprehensively licks her face as she lies there, screaming that she is being eaten alive and displaying an improbable amount of blue knicker. Thunder (howling all the time) takes unfair advantage of the tartan rug.

There is more.

It gets worse.

You are surrounded by huge, red-faced sweating men, on huge sweating horses which stamp and froth at you. One of the biggest and reddest-faced men bellows at you, demanding whether you have seen a ragged looking fellow pass this way, what? Bereft of speech, you point the way the runner has gone.

The whole ghastly crew go howling and growling and tootling away, the red-faced one in the lead.

Then of course there were the young couples who had paused in some secluded nook to discuss conceptual existentialism (I should not wonder) which everybody knows can only be properly understood in a state of, at least semi-, nudity. I do not know what being intimately licked by large black dogs and surrounded by red-faced men on horses does for your concepts. I can only tell you that the feedback we got on that occasion lacked what one might call the true philosophical approach to the problem.

So we continued our horrid chase until we ran down the runner in a hedgeback where he had collapsed with laughter. The Boot Hounds licked his face with joy and we all went back and had a drink.

That is the story of the Boot Hounds and an August evening that I could not but share with you.

But hold, there is an epilogue.

I had to get rid of the Boot Hounds. Their manners improved greatly but I could never get them steady with Men on Bicycles. Men on Bicycles would be pursued with tremendous cry, speed and enthusiasm until they would give a final terrified wobble and fall in a ditch — where, of course, they would get their faces comprehensively licked.

It became a bit of a problem. Luckily, a horse soldier friend of mine had a pack of Boot Hounds in Germany and thither mine went and were a great success.

I don't suppose anybody missed the odd German cyclist.

The beginning of this chapter talked about summer holidays and main roads in the west of England, and there's been the odd mention or three of dogs/hounds in the rest of the chapter, so I may as well bring August to an end by telling you a story (another permitted flash-back) which combined those elements — holidays, main roads and dogs, in this case a collie dog.

On the long road that winds its way into the Celtic

twilight of the west of Britain, there is a hill: a long and fairly steep hill with a right-handed bend halfway down it. On the outside of the bend there is a sharp drop into Mr Trevisick's field, which in turn descends steeply to the prattling little stream in the bottom.

At the top of the hill, there is a public house which is very likely called the Emmet Tump and which I used to frequent in the far off carefree days of my youth. Another frequenter of the pub was, and very likely still is, one Sid Perryman.

Sid was a sheep dealer which meant that he spent a lot of time going to markets and sales. On his way home it was his wont to park his lorry outside the Emmet with Dan his collie left in charge, whilst he went in for a stiffener.

Thus it happened one fine summer's afternoon as it had happened many times before, except that this time something of a distraction was hoving into view.

The distraction manifested itself in the person of Elvis, the resident labrador of the Emmet Tump, with whom Dan had long ceased to be on friendly terms. As soon as Elvis appeared round the corner of the pub, Dan leaped to the driver's window of the cab and commenced a torrent of abuse. Elvis being a chap with a written pedigree to support ignored this vulgar display and walking up to the offside front wheel of the lorry, he lifted his leg on it.

This obvious insult to Dan and his property was too much. Dan raged, he swore, he leaped about the cab screaming abuse at his rival. In so doing, he landed with undue force upon the ancient and definitely dodgy hand brake of the lorry and disengaged it. Sid had left the lorry on the brow of a hill because it was not only the handbrake that was suspect, the battery had known better days as well, and a run off was sometimes necessary.

Sid was just happily into his second pint when the landlord suggested that that might be his, Sid's, lorry that was just passing the window apparently being driven by a dog.

As one man, the inhabitants of the Four Ale Bar scrambled through the door and, sure enough, there was Sid's lorry trundling slowly and majestically down the hill on the wrong side of the road with Cap'n Dan on the bridge.

We should now leave the lorry to its trundling and the Four Ale Bar to its ineffectual and somewhat beer-gutted pursuit. We should switch our attention to the bottom of the hill.

At the bottom of the hill we shall find the family Perkins (the Sidcup Perkins, to distinguish them from any less well-known branches of the family) whom we shall find closely united in disharmony and a new Ford motor car. The disharmony stems from the fact that the enforced unit consists of Reginald and Marjorie Perkins (he driving and she navigating) whilst the back seat is fully occupied with Miss Sharon Perkins (7), Master Wayne Perkins (5) and Mrs Mavis Summers (don't ask) who is Mrs Perkins' mother. They have all been on a happy family holiday in a caravan at Portscatho. It rained the entire week. Wayne has had fairly consistent trots and Mrs Summers' "complaint" (don't ask) has been giving her gyp. The Back Seat has been in a state of poorly contained peevishness all the way from Redruth. Please do not point out that you would not go from Portscatho to Sidcup via Redruth. Mrs Perkins is sensitive about her navigating skills and Mr Perkins has been rather labouring this very point.

The mood in the Perkins Ford as it reached the left-handed bend on the hill can be best described as one of simmering discontent.

At this moment and place, they came face to face with Dan the collie and his lorry who were both, as you may remember, proceeding down the hill on the wrong side of the road. It was fortunate that Dan had not knocked the handbrake entirely off. The progress of the lorry was stately rather than speedy. The lorry met and embraced the car with much scrunching of metal and both vehicles came to a shuddering halt on the bend.

You will be relieved to hear that the only major casualty was the Perkins' car. Sid's lorry was old but sturdy and had suffered no more than superficial cuts and bruises. The only human physical casualty was Sharon Perkins who had the remains of her iced lolly embedded in her left nostril. It is true that Mrs Summers was having a "turn" but that was a normal part of any Perkins family outing.

To be fair, perhaps another major casualty was Mr Perkins, confronted with the steaming and crumpled remains of his proud new car.

He was Cross.

At this moment the Emmet Tump posse arrived, lamentably out of breath. Sid seized the hand that the speechless Mr Perkins was pointing at the disaster between his two enormous paws and began pumping it: "Bloody good job you was coming round the corner just then, boss. My bloody lorry would have gone right on over the bank. Could have been damaged too. Never mind. This is a proper job; a proper job."

There I think we might tactfully withdraw; do you not agree?

September

September is one of my favourite months. There comes a moment when one goes out of the door first thing in the morning and after scratching the crutch in the approved manner, one sniffs the air. There it is, that first something in the air, a certain sharpness, tang, crispy feeling: it is the first hint of autumn. I love the autumn: the colours, the light, the smells. Autumn on the Cheviots can be particularly lovely. Mind you, if it chooses to throw in some of those special gales that whizz across the Atlantic, turn left up the Irish Sea, make a right somewhere round the Mull of Galloway, and then really wind themselves up on the way across to Northumberland, then I cease to be so keen on autumn.

September is also one of my busiest months. The Backwoodsman will be very busy with cubhunting in September, which may well take up three days of his week. This leaves him with four days in which he has to buy, prepare for sale and sell sheep, who will also require an orgy of injecting, dosing and dipping. If he is a scribbling Backwoodsman, he will also have to cope with the importunate demands of Editors. All Editors appear to spend the entire summer in either Tuscany or the Auvergne, although some may return to shoot a grouse. September finds them back in their offices, mightily refreshed and invigorated and wanting 2,000 words yesterday, I should not wonder. You may feel that all this activity does not leave much time for the Backwoodsman to take his wife shopping. Backwoodsmen never take their wives shopping.

I can also judge the advent of autumn by watching the gradual emptying of the caravan park in the valley. I am always glad to see them go. Not, I hasten to add, that I have anything against caravanners; I could say that some of my best friends are caravanners, but it would be stretching the truth a bit. Although perhaps I should tell you about the General.

The General is not in the general run (rather good that, what?) of caravan owners. We were all rather surprised when he announced that he had purchased a caravan and how splendidly useful it was going to be for taking to three-day events and such like. We should all get one, he said. We all thought about this in silence. We had all experienced the General's driving, even if only vicariously. One should understand that the General was a very brave tank soldier during the Corporal Hitler unpleasantness, but what might be all right in the western desert is not necessarily what is required on modern roads. At last someone summoned up the courage to ask the General how he fared driving with a caravan hitched behind. I think we all had worrying visions of meeting him. Oh no, said the General, he never actually towed the thing himself: he understood they were bloody awful things to drive. No, he always sent a man on ahead with the caravan and drove down to wherever later with his wife. A marvellous idea, he said, couldn't think why we all did not do it.

But, we said, not everybody had men to send on. Stuff and nonsense, said the General, we all had wives and/or girl friends, did we not? We should send them on with the caravan; get some use out of them. Well, you must admit that he does have a point.

But I digress: the reason that I am always glad to see the back of the caravans is that there is usually a litter of cubs down behind the caravan site and the emptying of the park means that we shall soon be able to get amongst them.

However, first we must turn our attention to more pressing matters: like sheep sales.

I do not know how many million sheep flow out of Northumberland during the autumn, but the figure must be considerable. The Borders is justly renowned for the excellence both of its stock and its stockmen. For many of them, the autumn sales represent their main source of income for the year. It is their harvest. Good sales can mean the difference between solvency and not.

So September is the time of sales. I usually take my lambs to my local mart which is just up the road. Sometimes I go a bit further away if there is a special sale which I think might attract large numbers of buyers. It is a bit of a lottery, frankly. You just have to be in the right place on the right days: sounds easy, does it not?

There are "fat sales", but we are not supposed to mention fat any more: cholesterol, you see; I suppose we ought to say "finished (ready for the butcher) lamb sales". Anyway these are the lambs that go straight to be killed. Now I do not want to hear any of you out there wittering on about "Red Meat being bad for you"; that is a lot of pinko nonsense. All Backwoodsmen consume huge quantities of red meat; makes us the fine strapping, moustache-twirling buckos that we are, what? We also eat lots of salmon to keep the grey matter in trim, but that is another story.

Back to the sales. There are sales for "store lambs": these go south to lusher pastures where they can be finished away from the biting winds and shrivelled herbage of the north. There are sales for "ewes and ewe lambs" and last, but by no means least, because without them the whole process would grind to a halt, there are sales of "tups" (rams).

All the main sales are crammed into a six-week period with September in the middle of it.

Many farmers love going to sales and marts. They regard them as a jolly as well as business. They can catch up on the gossip from a wide catchment area. Old friendships can be reaffirmed and old enmities freshened up. Marts bring little gladness to my soul. If I could find a better way of marketing my produce, then I would grasp it enthusiastically.

Marts are cold, boring and uncomfortable. Just suppose that you have a pen of forty lambs to sell and there are some seven thousand lambs at the sale; it is a guinea to a gooseberry that you are going to be spending a big part of the day sitting about waiting for your turn. Marts are not user-friendly places. The order of selling is balloted; at least that is what the auctioneers will tell you and of course I believe them. It is purely fortuitous that the lambs belonging to the Mart Chairman always occupy a prime slot in the selling order. There is no point in being a leading and very shrewd agriculturalist if you cannot help your luck along a bit.

You do not want to be in the ring too early because the buyers often take a little time to warm up. They do not want to appear too eager and, besides, they tell themselves there are almost certainly better things to come. Neither do you want to be at the end; most of the buyers will have gone home by then and the dealers will nail you to the rostrum.

No, you want to be somewhere in the early middle — unless, of course, the trade collapses about then, in which case you would have been better at the beginning. Or again, one of the big dealers might get a telephoned order from a down-country buyer in which case trade will suddenly take fire just after you have donated your lambs to charity.

It is all very trying and difficult and the best thing you

can probably do is to go and get some refreshment. There may be two alternatives: the Drovers' Arms or the Mart Caff. In the Drovers you will get whisky which will taste more or less like whisky; in the Mart Caff you will get coffee that does not. Which would you prefer? Well, if you insist, although I'm not much of a one for drinking in the daytime normally. Before we go any further, I must bring something important to your attention. It is an immutable rule, laid down by the Clerk of the Weather, that all marts shall take place in pouring rain.

By the time we shoulder our way into the bar of the Drovers, the room is bulging at the seams. The atmosphere is of such a consistency that, should you so wish, you could cut it into chunks, wrap it up and take it home with you. It is an interesting mixture of tobacco, wet oilskins, sheep, sheep shit, wet collie dog and highly-seasoned shepherd: mix well and add plenty of alcohol to taste.

All around is a roar of conversation through which you will have to elbow your way to the bar. I could see you were a little confused when you asked for a Scotch and got asked whether you wanted a pint or a half? Scotch here means Scottish Bitter Beer. Whisky comes in nips (small) or drams (large) and thank you very much, I do not mind if I do.

Snatches of conversation:

"Yon's a muckle hard fearm, I doubt: winter nine months of the year and bad weather the other three."

" 'Sic' a grand aad dog, I'm telling yer, he was by Geordie's Jock, who was by Jimmy's Moss, who was by Matty's Scott, who was by . . ."

In the corner two Yorkshiremen are supping cautious

pints and smoking cautious whiffs. One drops his whiff on the well-manured floor, retrieves it and continues to smoke. Then he turns to his companion: "Has thoo ever smoked a cigar covered in sheep shit?"

Pause: "Nay; cassn't say I have."

"Doesn't taste ower good," but he smokes to the (I should think very) bitter end.

I think it is high time we got back to the sale. Back down the rows of pens we go to see how my poor lambs are surviving in the steady downpour. They are looking miserable which is only to be expected. The only comfort is that all the other lambs will be looking equally miserable. Farmers and shepherds are leaning on their sticks by the pens keeping a weather eye open for signs of buyers. Rumours will flicker round the pens about the presence, or absence, of the big buyers from Yorkshire and the Midlands: they can make or mar the trade. Six thousand store lambs should turn over something like £250,000 and everybody wants a slice of the pie.

The start of the sale will be announced by a man walking round ringing a handbell or, if the mart is modernised, there will be a tannoy system which will announce: "Whistle, bleep, crackle, bleep, RING ONE!"

The sale ring is like an amphitheatre, with the auctioneer's rostrum facing the semi-circle of rising tiers of seats. They are wood; hard, mud-stained wood which will cater impartially for your bottom, or the manure-caked boots of the man behind. Marts are not a place for your designer suitings.

Most of the big buyers will group themselves at the ringside where a twitch of a finger, the droop of an eyelid, or the merest wag of a catalogue, will catch the expert eye of the auctioneer. Or auctioneers, for they will work in relays throughout the seven, eight, or nine hours that a big sale can take.

Each lot comes into the ring according to its place in the draw accompanied by the owner, the shepherd and sometimes, it seems, the whole family. The market drovers, who are often retired shepherds, will be working feverishly leading up to and taking away from the ring, so that the flow is never interrupted.

"Lot 153, gentlemen, from Mr Why of Starveasy, right off the heather tops, bound to go on; there's a fine bunch of lambs; look at the grand skins on them; what'll you say for them? Stand on? (That is to start bidding at the selling price of the last lot: you should get so lucky.) What'll you give for them then? Thirty-eight? Thirty-seven, then? Start them somebody! Thirty-five bid — thirty-six — half — thirty-seven — thirty-eight — I'll take a half — half bid — thirty-nine — you're out at the back, sir. (He does not like it; he's shaking his head.) Forty, thank you sir — forty-one — half — any more? Right, I'm selling then at forty-one fifty — Bang! — Smith 2. (Bought by Mr Smith who wants them in his second lorry load and has indicated as much by twitching two fingers.) Thank you, Jim (Mr Why)," and Mr Why and his lambs leave the ring and part company for ever.

I always feel rather a prune in the ring. I have to admit to something of a pang when I see my lambs being driven away. After all I have lavished a great deal of tender loving care on them; seen them born, helped them to their first suck, helped to see the maternal bond firmly established, prevented them hanging themselves on wire fences and from drowning themselves in water troughs. My stockmanship has brought them, alive, bright and healthy, to the sale ring where hard-bitten men have been motivated to bid good money for them. It does not do for a stock farmer to get too sentimental about his charges. After all Sentiment will not be one of the things that the bank manager will take into account when he reviews my overdraft. So the pang is quickly replaced by relief as I set off to the office to collect my cheque.

It is usually my custom to leave a little "luck" money in the office for the purchaser: it is a pleasant enough old custom, but it has to be said that some buyers will go to immense lengths to extract it. One of these is Mr Swadlincote who just happens to have bought my lambs. I have a little mental bet with myself that I shall not reach the office unmolested. I am right.

There is a sound of aggravated wheezing and large pounding feet behind me. "Young man! I say, young man!" I turn round. It is Mr Swadlincote: he is a Big Dealer in every possible way and therefore not the best of movers. Nevertheless, he is waddling and puffing at best pace and obviously in the grip of strong emotion. "Now then, young man, I bought them lambs of yours, tha knows. Aye, and gave a tidy price for 'em too. Tha'll be giving me a bit back on 'em, for Luck like." I sigh deeply and get out my wallet. I am always amazed at the lengths men like Mr Swadlincote, who must turn over many thousands of pounds every week and retain a good few as they flow past, will go to to get an extra fiver off a miserable punter like me.

Ah well, time for a cup of tea.

September is also the time of my favourite hound show. Just suppose that you felt impelled to follow the course of the old Roman Dere Street. Somewhere in the wild hills you would come to a crossroads on a windswept moor. It is a desolate place apart from a corner of a ruined stone building, and a wood-and-tarpaper shack which you may be surprised to discover is, in fact, a village hall.

This is the setting for my favourite show — although it is not really much of a show. Four packs bring a few hounds and there will be a select showing of sheep. In the village hall there will be a produce show and you can do no better than to buy one of the cakes. There is nothing else, except a trestle table set up in the angle of the ruined building, above which a ragged tarpaulin flaps in the perennial gale and gives an illusion of shelter. Stacked in the corner behind the table will be rank upon rank of cardboard boxes. These boxes contain the reason for this show being held: bottles of whisky. As to why it is held at this place, the reason is again simple. The local water is held to be of such especial excellence that it is worth bringing the whisky to this barren spot to mix with it.

The showing is dealt with briskly and as soon as it is over, everyone rubs their hands with relief and sets off in the direction of the tarpaulin.

The one thing I never do is to attempt to drive home from this show. The way home lies through a town notorious for enthusiastic breathalysers.

I once persuaded my Senior Joint Master to drive me to the show which he reluctantly agreed to do, having extracted a promise of maximum good behaviour and coming when I was called. Well of course, I did not. I fell among thieves: they brutally forced whisky upon me; they stripped my good intentions from me and trampled them under their tackety boots.

Every so often a fluttered messenger would appear and proclaim the increasing grief of my Senior Joint Master at my non-appearance (he had been promised crumpets for tea, you see). "Howway man, the aad gadgie's lowpin up an doon: he'll wedge ye if ye divvin dee what yor telt." From which I got the impression that Sir Caspar was contemplating physical violence if he was kept from his crumpets one minute more. But of course just at that crucial moment another large dram would be thrust into my hand and . . . Sir Caspar has subsequently declined to escort me to the show.

As the autumn afternoon drifts into evening, it becomes increasingly obvious to me that home is where I am not going to get tonight. I shall go up the valley. The big hill farms up the valley keep open house the night after the show. A wandering foxhunter will find food, laughter, song, good conversation and possibly just another smidgen of whisky. Somewhere there will also be a place to lay my head for the night, or what will be left of it.

One memorable night I stopped between farms, a strange drowsiness having suffused my senses and I thought that I would take a little nap in the back of my van. I was rudely awakened by banging on the side of the van and a battery of faces staring in the back. I forgot to mention that there is also a dance in the tarpaper shack. The dance had ended and the shepherds were heading for the hills.

"Whit is it?"

"Whaat's a deein?"

"It's Wully."

"Whisht man, the buggor's deid."

"Haddaway-man, he's no deid; he's gyezend (thirsty)."

"Tyek a haad on him; we'll tak him to wor hoose."

Howwaay man, and divvnt cowp yer boilie." With this last, timely injunction that I was not to be sick on my rescuers, I was laid corpse-like across several broad shoulders and borne to the cottage where I was revived with restoring draughts of, well would you believe, whisky?

October

October is another of my favourite months. In a good
"back end" it can be a month of extraordinary loveli-
ness on the Cheviots. There may well be a touch of
frost rime in the early mornings and you can feel the air
reaming out the lungs. By midday there will be pleasant
warmth in the sun, but there will always be that edge to
the air that tells you that this is autumn and that you
will be glad of a fire come evening.

On the hills the brackens are dying. The hillsides are swathes of intermingling colours: green, brown, purple, gold, black and all sorts of subtle variations thereon.

For me, just being in the hills is a pleasure. To sit on a sun-warmed rock and allow the eye to be led naturally from one rollingly voluptuous hill to another until they blur into the purple distance. To watch the cloud shadows racing on the fell side across the valley, scattered with white dots of sheep.

A shrill but distant whistle and a scattered shout break the mood. The sheep are starting to bunch. There is a black-and-white dog snaking through the bents above them. Far down the fell is a matchstick-sized figure which the binoculars turn into Black Sykes Willy, whistling complicated commands through his fingers to Moss, high above him. No one but Willy would want to whistle through Willy's fingers, I might add.

The sheep are running on the other corner of the hill. That will be Willy's man Donald coming round the far hillend with his dogs.

Black Sykes is gathering, which is a timely reminder that the hills are a place of work and that not everyone can sit mooning on a rock. Come with me on a Gather.

We established earlier that it does not take too long to gather my little farm, but sometimes I go and give the Blacks of Longhope a hand. The Brothers Black farm the top end of a long lonely valley which gives its name to the farm. One side of the valley rises to 2,500 feet; the other side can manage no better than a miserable 2,300 feet. If you come down one side you might just find enough level ground to balance precariously for a minute before setting off up the other side.

At one time the farm needed six shepherds to herd it. Thanks to the Shepherding Bike, the place is now run with the two brothers, Tim and seventeen dogs.

Even so, a little extra help is welcome for a gather.

Picture, if you will, a hillside. It is steep; almost sheer in places. It is covered in heather, bracken and boulders. It is cut about with steep-sided boggy-bottomed "sykes" or small valleys. It is rent with rushing, rock-bedizened hill streams. It is about three miles long and its top end is shrouded in semi-permanent cloud.

This not especially fetching place is home for a cut of wild black face ewes. They are "heifed" to that bit of hill, that is, they are born and brought up there. They have no intention of leaving it. However, several times a year they have to be brought down to the farm for general repairs and maintenance and to have their lambs drawn for sale. The ewes take exception to what they conceive as an unpardonable intrusion in their routine and a gross infringement of their civil liberties. Therefore, they will do everything they can to prevent themselves and their lambs being included in the gather. They will twist and turn, hide, bolt, double back, sulk, and run in ever-decreasing circles until they apparently do the impossible and disappear. A hillside dotted with sheep will suddenly be empty.

What is needed for this sort of gather is man and dog power. The brothers are admirers of barking dogs for gathering sheep: they own a New Zealand Huntaway which works in a rather similar manner to my Australian Kelpie. So when they have a big gather, Oz and I often get invited. We both look forward to it: change of routine, you see.

The cool of the day is the time to gather. So we usually

arrive at the farm in time for a cup of tea.

After tea the farm contingent set off on their motorcycles, each surrounded by a cloud of collies. These hillsides are too steep and too rough to allow the use of a four-wheeler. Much fine gold would not tempt me to attempt to ride a two-wheeler along those precipices, but the Blacks do it every day as a matter of course and make it look easy: it is not.

I drive my pick-up along the strew of boulders that passes as a track until I reach the old steading far up the valley. That is as far as Rupert will take me. Oz comes out of the back of the pick-up like a Champagne cork and bounces round me with enthusiasm: he loves his work.

The "path" to the head of the valley follows the stream up from the steading, and the valley is narrowing all the time to a steep narrow V. There is a ragged cloud cap on the tops to my right and somewhere up in the cloud I can very faintly hear the sound of a motorbike.

Up on a crag a raven is complaining. The occasional grouse bursts out of the heather urging me to "Go Back! Go Back!": push off.

There will be the occasional ewe and lamb, or small group, down by the burnside. They glare at me and then set away up the hill at a determined trot, the lambs trailing behind. I shout and wave my stick to urge them on their way. The more I can push them up into the middle of the hillside the better. The rough uneven ground on the burnside provides a great chance for a wily old ewe to outwit the dogs and break back to freedom.

My spot is a large boulder at the point where a little hill stream tumbles down into the main burn. It is now a question of waiting and fending off the midges with slaps, smoke and pungent lotion.

All is silence except for the burbling of the burn.

A faint and distant shout comes from far up the hill and some faint but constant barking. Oz is suddenly all attention, his ears cocked and body tense.

Five hundred feet above, a line of sheep comes cascading down a steep trod. The shouting and whistling is nearer, and an embicycled figure appears, picking its way down the trod.

Scattered lines of sheep are moving all along the face now, converging and mingling as they come slowly down the valley. It is here, in the thick bracken beds, that the maximum pressure is needed to keep the flock moving. It is here that the sheep will become sullen and seek to break back to the hill. It is here that Oz and I come into play.

An old ewe picks up her skirts, calls to her lamb and makes a determined bolt for the rocky stream bed.

Oz heads her neatly, barks in her face and restores her to the paths of righteousness.

Men and dogs form a rough line along the hill face. High above, the Huntaway is barking the sheep out of a bracken bed. It is noise that keeps them moving.

I notice a bunch of ewes sulking in the brackens below me. "Speak up, Oz! speak up!" The little brown dog disappears like a bullet into the bracken.

"Owf! Owf! Owf!" and the sheep begin to move. "Owf! Owf! Owf!" They are away now, swelling the long skeins of sheep threading their way all along the hillside.

The evening is still and muggy, the sheep are "gey dour" and the dogs are tiring in the hot and airless bracken beds.

"Ho! Ho! Ho! Shift you old buggers."

"Come by, Scott! Come bye!"

"PheeeEEEugh! LAY DOON!"

"Speak up, Oz! Speak up!"

"Owf! Owf! Owf!"

Men and dogs are closing in now and the sheep are being gradually forced into a main bunch. The air is heavy with the complaint of worried mothers and lost lambs.

When we are well down the valley, a wire fence denotes a return to relative civilization. The sheep are pouring through an open gate. Frantic lambs try to break back and are neatly fielded by the dogs. At last the gate is shut. The blaring flock moves away, reassembling its scattered family units. The dogs stretch out panting and weary. The men lean on their sticks and mop their brows. There is little man- or dog-power left.

Someone says that it is time for some supper and maybe a dram. Now, that is the nicest thing that anyone has said to me today.

Autumn hunting continues, of course. We have some long hard days in October, there being plenty of daylight available.

Let me tell you of one particular day that sticks in my memory. This happened back in the days when I was still hunting hounds.

I was riding a new horse and the ladies had been very insistent that he was not to have too long a day. We had met at seven a.m. and had had a busy morning (about five hours) and I thought that that would just nicely do him.

I was riding down the hill in a comfortable unbuttoned sort of mood thinking of breakfast on a flask of tea and bacon sandwich and how good the horse had been, how marvellous my hounds were and what an absolutely spiffing huntsman I was, when old Pagan who was investigating a patch of bracken went "*WOOF!*" and out of the bracken shot the biggest fox you ever did see.

"*WHOOPEE!* " howled my hounds who were supposed to be tired.

"Oh shit!" said the Spiffing Huntsman, mentally discarding his flask and sarnies because the hounds had turned away from the direction of civilization, horse boxes and tea and were heading out into our most wild and trackless country.

I will not bore you with details of our scramble through the hideous peat hags of Cushat Law and Sting Head. Let me not harrow you with tales of our tribulations amongst the afforested precipices of Hog Lairs and Whiteburnshank. Suffice it to say that on our jaded horses we had no chance of staying anywhere near hounds; it was only the shepherds on their motorbikes who were able to stay in contention. Every now and then a fluttered messenger would roar up to gabble an account and give us new directions before squirting away in a shower of mud and a belch of smoke.

On and on we struggled through 7,000 acres of forestry, out the other side, across a precipitous valley and up a long long hill. We had seen and heard nothing for ages but when we breasted the top of the hill, hope rekindled. There far across the valley was a line of toy bikes whizzing along and just in front of them a polka of white dots was disappearing into a little wood.

It was down hill all the way and my unfortunate horse did manage some sort of trot, but the fox was killed and eaten before we got there. I made it an eight-mile point, but as the hounds and the bikes went it was thirty-seven miles.

Not really an average cubhuting day but then the great thing about hunting is that you never quite know what is going to happen.

On occasion I go a-knackering.

Hounds require a great deal of protein to keep them in good working fettle and part of that protein comes from flesh.

I do not suppose that many of you have given the matter much thought, but if you would now give the matter some consideration you will perceive that to open tins of Doggy Dins for sixty hounds would not only be hard on the wrist, it would also be murder on the exchequer. There has to be another method of obtaining toothsome red meat.

Then suppose that you are a farmer and you come out one morning with your hair in a braid (metaphorical) and a song in your heart only to find that dear old Buttercup has handed in her dinner pail during the night and is lying in a ditch with all four legs in the air.

It is quite natural that your first feeling is one of sorrow, tinged with financial regret. Your next reaction is to ask yourself what to do with the mortal husk of a deceased cow. I mean, have you ever considered the size of the hole that you would have to dig?

What most farmers do is to telephone the local hunt kennels. In a fairly short time, a neat little man in a brown smock will appear with a Land-Rover and a trailer equipped with a winch. Buttercup will be hauled aboard, covered with a tarpaulin and in a very short time will have disappeared from your farm and balance sheet.

Back at the kennels, Buttercup will be skinned and cut up. Very soon all her edible portions will be simmering nicely in a huge copper, well on the way to becoming the Plat de Jour and the source of canine protein with which we started by worrying about.

Most hunts operate this knackering service. It helps the farmers; it helps the hunt and it provides a constant source of contact between the two which is of inestimable value.

In the old days, most hunts would have kept a full-time knackerman who would have spent the whole day on the road with a horse and cart. One hunt I was connected with had had such a man and for many years he was a familiar sight on the country roads with his cart pulled by a huge mule called Jasper. The old man died suddenly and only then was Jasper's peculiarity discovered. There was absolutely no way that Jasper would pass a pub; he would stop resolutely at every one and refuse to budge. It was eventually discovered that if he were taken into the pub yard, driven round and out again, he would then proceed quite happily, but he would never never go straight past.

Nowadays the Jaspers have been replaced by motor vehicles, but the old style of knackermen still exist and still ply their trade with relish.

It is not really surprising that knackering might give a chap a thirst. It is surprising, however, that knackermen often seemed to have considerable success with the ladies.

This is even more surprising when you consider the effluvia that work of this sort imparts to the person and the clothing. A man has to have considerable charm to overcome a handicap like that. I even remember one man who used to claim his numerous victims in the back of this truck: bouncing about on the sheep carcasses.

I would not want you to think that the above is in any way autobiographical. I do not have that sort of charm.

But I used to enjoy knackering: bodging about the byways and calling in at farms and hearing all the local gossip as one worked the winch.

You can have too much of a good thing, however. As a young master/huntsman I used to look after my own hounds and do all the knackering. In a busy time this meant starting at 0600 and very often be still working at 0100 the next morning. That can be a bit wearing. But even unpaid overtime can have its moments.

One night after hunting I had gone out to a farm high up in the hills to pick up a big (very dead) Scottish blackface ram: they are the ones with the big curly horns. To fortify myself for another night of skinning, I called in at a lonely moorland pub on the way home. I groaned a bit when I saw a large and expensive car amongst the agricultural-type vehicles in the car park. It was Cuthbert's car. Cuthbert was a pain. It was his custom to drive out from the town and patronise (and I use the word advisedly) this comfortable little pub and its comfortable clientele. It was quite obvious at a glance that Cuthbert was in more than usually poisonous form that night. He had spread his considerable bulk along the entire length of the bar and the wretched locals were huddled in a corner, rather like a collective rabbit mesmerised by a stoat. Cuthbert bought me a drink. Cuthbert bought everybody drinks whether they were willing or not. He then began once more to entertain his captive audience.

There was a tug at the back of my coat. Reg whispered as he asked if I had got anything in the truck? I told him: well now, that was a proper job, he said, would I meet them outside.

Cuthbert boomed on as Jack, Reg and I sidled out of the door. We sat the big tup on the back seat of Cuthbert's car and it seemed only right to put the rug across its lower legs.

Cuthbert blossomed in the unusual hospitality that he received that night and was booming more loudly than ever as we escorted him to his car at closing time and helped him into his seat; we waved him goodbye.

The road from the pub went sharply down hill through a series of hairpin bends girded with stone walls.

We all waited expectantly.

We did not hear the scream, but we heard the crash.

Well, what do you do if, on rounding a bend, alone in your car, somebody taps you on the shoulder. Then you turn round to see a black face with staring eyes and enormous horns apparently leaning over to have a confidential chat? What do you do? Scream and bend your car round a stone wall, that is what you do. You will very likely be gibbering a bit when strong hands come to pull you forth. You will gesticulate and froth a bit and point to the hideous form that accosted you. A hideous horned being? What? Where? And sure enough there is nothing to be seen, just a pair of tail lights on the road that leads over the moors to the kennels and a strange smell of corruption that is hanging about the back seat of the car.

The moor is a strange place at night. There have been many happenings there that defy rational explanation.

In the autumn my thoughts sometimes turn to fishing. I am not a fisherman within the meaning of the act. Many Backwoodsmen are keen piscators and like nothing better than being immersed to the armpits in the Tweed doing a Spey Roll, I should not wonder. They will drive to some remote part of Wester Ross and wander about weighed down with rods, line boxes, six-tier cases of flies, luncheon hampers, flasks, priests, ghillies, nets and the most frightful social gaffs. There is either too little water and no fish, or there is too much water and no fish. All in all, it sounds an awful waste of time to me. I have not got the time, or the patience, to muck about like that. I am sure that the scenery is wonderful but I have got all the scenery I want just outside my back door.

When I want to go fishing I ring up my friend Geordie.

Geordie and Bob are brothers. They are professional fishermen. Their family have been fishing off the same Northumberland beach for 500 years. In the summer they fish for sea trout and in the autumn it is the lobsters.

It is pitch black when I arrive at the beach with just a faint greying on the eastern horizon. There are already lights on some of the boats in the little bay and the steady chunky throb of a big marine diesel.

As the eyes become accustomed to the gloom, the shapes of men can be seen moving purposefully about the darkened beach. A match flares and the first fag of the day heralds some early coughing.

A tractor coughs and chokes in sympathy and then its engine springs to life. You may have wondered where all the old Fordson Major and Nuffield Tractors went to. The answer is that they are alive and well (if a trifle bronchitic) and living on the fishing beaches of the north-east, where they haul the boats and fish boxes to and fro.

Bob and the tractor come chugging out of the darkness, with the dinghy on the trailer, and down to the water's edge. The trailer is backed in until the dinghy can be slid off into the water. Boxes, fuel cans and other gear are loaded.

As a great privilege, I am allowed to take the oars and row out across the little harbour to where the *Lorna Cordelia* lies at her moorings.

The *Lorna* (after Geordie's daughter) *Cordelia* ("Daughter of the Sea") is a typical East Coast coble: a boat made for working off the beach. The design harks back to the boats of the old Norse invaders: high, sharp stem and a square stern.

The *Lorna Cordelia* is 33 feet long and open, except where a tarpaulin awning is rigged forrard to keep off the worst of the weather. She is made in the traditional way: clinker built with larch planking: the ribs are oak.

There is a grey sky by the time we reach the coble and off-load ourselves and the gear from the dinghy. The Perkins Marine Diesel gasps, splutters and settles down to a comforting steady hump. The moorings are slipped and we creep out of the harbour on the half-flood tide.

The brothers go to the pots six days a week in the season (weather permitting). In the autumn they drop the pots fairly close inshore but as the weather gets colder the lobsters retreat to deeper water and the boats have to follow. There are eight lines of pots with thirty pots each. The pots lie on the seabed attached to a long line which has a marker buoy at each end.

There is a nice oily swell running as we chug out into the grey early morning sea. I know from experience that my internal workings can take grave exception to a nice oily swell. Matters may not be improved by the fact that I am sharing the midships thwart with several boxes of very deceased mackerel which will shortly have to be cut up into nice handy chunks for baiting the pots. I discuss the matter with the internal plumbing department which decides to figuratively shrug its shoulders on this occasion.

You may have been struck by the lack of dialogue in this piece. The cold grey North Sea in the early morning and a heavy diesel thumping alongside are not conducive to conversation. It is better to be quiet, to smell the evocative smells of boat and sea, and to watch the day come creeping over the Northumberland coast.

We reach the first marker. The engine is cut. The buoy is brought inboard with a boat hook and the brothers swing into action with the skilled precision of a well-trained team.

In the old days the pots were hauled by hand, but now there is a knacky little motor winch. Bob works the winch and as each pot comes inboard, he passes it over to Geordie. With nimble, practised fingers Geordie unlaces the twine-closed side of the pots and removes the contents. Then the old bait is flicked out and new (fresh?) bait is placed inside. Agile fingers lace up the side of the pot again.

The empty pots are stacked in strict order on the starboard side. When the haul is complete, Geordie takes the helm, the boat is put slow ahead and Bob feeds the pots overboard, always with the tide. To haul and relay the single line of pots takes anything up to an hour.

And what is in the pots? Lobsters? Yes, certainly lobsters. The size of a takeable lobster is strictly controlled: it has to measure 85mm from the eye socket to the back of the head. The first grading is done by eye. Anything obviously under-age is returned to the sea. Something like sixty percent of the catch is returned. The takeable ones go into a box where they are covered in layers of damp sacking.

All sorts and conditions of minor marine life also appear in the pots: starfish, spiny sea urchins, yummy-looking whelks (no market for them in the UK), hermit crabs who, having no shell of their own, move into vacant whelk shells, moving from shell to shell as they increase their size. There are myriads of different sorts of little crab, all of which Geordie has a name for and lots of strange small fish, "puddlers", "John Dories" and so forth. All these uninvited guests get returned alive to the deep with one exception: the octopus. Lobster fishermen hate octopi for the very good reason that they kill lobsters. Sure enough in one pot there is an octopus wrapped round a lobster. The lobster is still just alive but the octopus has already torn one claw off, so the wretch gets short shrift. With a deft movement, Geordie turns it inside out, rather as one does a sock, and hoys the thing overboard.

By now it is full grey daylight. The details of the coastline a mile distant are now plain to see. All around on the grey crawling sea other boats can be seen about the same business. To the north are the boats from Craster and Seahouses and to the south those from Amble. Each boat moves attended by its own cloud of shrieking squabbling gulls, for whom this must be a valuable source of breakfast.

It takes five or six hours to lift all the pots and throughout the brothers work steadily, sustained by nothing more than peppermints.

But now it is time for home. The Backwoodsman is allowed to take the helm, whilst the Brothers sort methodically through the catch. Each lobster is carefully measured with a special gauge and those that fail to make 85mm go back to the sea to grow some more. Each lobster kept has its claws carefully secured with elastic bands to stop them damaging each other in the box. The claws are not for show: one for holding and one for chewing. Cock lobsters can do each other some nasty mischief.

The *Lorna Cordelia* comes to rest on her moorings. Then it is into the dinghy and back to the beach where the precious morning's take is put on the tractor and taken up to the communal shed. Each boat's catch is weighed and left ready for the daily collection by the lorry from the Fisherman's Cooperative at Eyemouth. From there the lobsters go to France, Spain — and a few to restaurants in Britain. For all you know, that lobster you enjoyed in Paris (at great expense) was put in its wet sacking by a Northumbrian Backwoodsman. This must add to its interest and flavour for you and make it a cheap feed at double the price.

All this talk of feed brings me back to the fact that back

on the beach it is now *c*1130. I have been up since 0430; six hours heaving about in the bosom of the deep and I am quite frankly jolly hungry. Not to worry; Geordie's wife Jean knows exactly how to fettle a salt-sharpened appetite — with relays of bacon, eggs, sausages, fried potatoes and toast, all washed down with gallons of hot strong tea. And if alongside the cup of tea there should appear just a nip of something restorative that is a matter between Geordie and me and absolutely nothing to do with anyone else.

November

As this chapter is November you might expect that it would be entirely devoted to the slaughter of pheasants and the pursuit of foxes, both being things that loom large in the Backwoodsman's winter plan. You will not get a great deal about pheasants from me because I do not shoot. I think that the only place for a pheasant is on my sideboard in a nicely roasted condition, whilst I salivate and strop the knife.

There will be a certain amount about hunting, but just to be annoying, I thought that I would start with something else. Let us consider singing.

All true Backwoodsmen sing, even if only in the bath. In case your imagination becomes fevered at the thought of chanting, naked Backwoodsmen just wait a bit; we will return to matters lavatorial later on. I am not suggesting that Backwoodsmen necessarily sing very well. Their repertoire may be limited to "Jolly boating weather tumty tumty tum", or half-remembered snatches from College Chapel like the bit about "The rich man in his castle, the poor man at his gate, God made them high and lowly, and ordered their estate", what the Backwoodsman would refer to as "good old-fashioned stuff with a proper tune; none of this modern, pinko, caterwauling, what?"

I also sing in the bath. There is something particularly pleasing about the acoustics of most bathrooms; something to do with the tiles and the steam, I suppose. However, I do not confine my efforts to the bathroom. I am a compulsive singer especially when under the mellowing effects of a drop of the right stuff. In fact the problem is not to get me singing: more one of getting me to stop. Not that I can see why anybody should wish me to stop as I have a particularly pleasing light baritone voice.

So what, you are going to ask me, do I sing? I sing traditional songs. I collect traditional songs and, in due course, commit them upon my public. Let me hold up my hand and caution you at this point. I can hear some of you clever Herberts out there saying wisely, "Ah, Folk Songs": absolutely not. Folk Songs are things committed by bearded men and women with hairy legs in Polytechnic Nasal and tambourines: not the same thing at all.

My repertoire is very eclectic. I can make you chuckle with "Tavistock Goosey Fair", or the "Threshing Machine". I can stroke your nostalgia with "Spansel Hill", or "The Wild Mountain Thyme". I can make you greet for all the things that might have been with "Maggie", and "The Old Rustic Bridge by the Mill". But my favourite oeuvre is undoubtedly "The Doosing of the Hoggs". This is a very old Northumbrian song and experts tell me that it is unique in its musical structure, being part song and part recitation. Be that as it may, it is rarely heard these days because there are very few people left who can sing it and I am proud to be numbered amongst that select band. I have only heard one other person sing it and he was the man from whom I learnt it. The song has a splendid dirge-like character that exactly fits the mood at some stage during almost any evening and should be committed with the eyes closed and a glass in at least one hand.

Now let us turn our attention to hunting. 1 November is the official start of the foxhunting season. Most hunts hold their opening meet on, or close to, 1 November.

The Opening Meet: now there is an evocative phrase. In those two words are hidden such jangling of nerves, such fraying of tempers, such polishing, boning, plaiting, frantic telephoning as the outsider would not believe.

The opening meet is the first formal occasion of the hunting season and everything and everybody has to look their best. Horses should be fit, sleek and shining. It is inevitable that their manes will be plaited. For thirty years I fought a war of attrition with my stable staff since it has always been my opinion that plaiting is a complete waste of time. Time which might be much better spent on other things. It is also my opinion that a good-looking horse does not need to be embellished by a plaited mane, and that it makes a common horse look more common. I proclaim loudly that a hogged (crew cut) mane is the smartest of all: always provided that a little scalp lock is left for me to hang onto when humping a fence or going up a steep hill.

Every year I would order "absolutely no plaits". This would be greeted with screams or pouts from the female staff. Old-fashioned male stud grooms would touch their caps and say "very good, sir, no plaits". Nevertheless when Tyrone, or Trendsetter, was pulled out of the box for me to get on, the mane would be trussed up like a corn dolly and all the stable staff would be looking at the far horizon as though expecting the imminent arrival of a flight of angels.

Everybody should look as smart as possible at the opening meet. This happy effect cannot be achieved overnight; a fact that many hunting people forget.

Let us take the boot, for instance. You should be able to shave by the mirror-like shine of your boot (or something equivalent if you are female) and this means boning. My bootmaker showed me how to bone a boot. I am probably one of the few people left in the British Isles who knows how to do it properly. The effect is incomparable. The fact that the boots will be covered in mud within moments of moving off is neither here nor there. The effect on morale of a shining boot is incalculable;

a fact that has not been lost on the British Army.

Everybody relates to a good turn out. A scruffy hunt soons gets a scruffy reputation. However, to appear at a meet with the correct mixture of lustrous red, gleaming white, and shining black requires much time spent in preparation. You cannot dig out your kit the night before the opening meet and try to remove last season's scars and mud in one hectic cleaning session. Nor is it any good frantically pulling on breeches and coat on the great morning to find suddenly that in some strange way everythng has shrunk during the summer. A day that starts to the accompaniment of popping safety pins is not likely to be a success.

You will not catch a Backwoodsman out like that. Backwoodsmen are sticklers for turn out. Should you meet a Backwoodsman bodging round the farm at home, you might think that he is doing a very good impersonation of Worzel Gummidge. I have heard of ignorant persons who have been so far misled in these circumstances as to address the mobile heap of rags as "my man": it is not an error they are likely to fall into twice.

However that is at home. When the Backwoodsman appears in Public he usually appears in full rig for the occasion — whatever it may be. His kit may not be new, indeed it may have been worn by his grandfather, but it will be correct in every detail and will be pressed and polished to the limit of human endeavour.

Some Backwoodsmen may be fortunate enough still to be in the possession of an Old Retainer. When I say "in the possession of" I mean just that. No one who has ever seen an Old Retainer functioning on all cylinders can have any doubt as to who is in charge.

"No, Sir John, I do not think the Houndstooth is quite what we want. I think the worsted with the self-effacing check is much more suitable. This tie will go very nicely, I think." You may think that I exaggerate but I can assure you that Jeeves still exists, albeit as an endangered species in the British Isles.

I do remember, however, running into one of the species who was in a high state of excitement and unhappiness. It seemed that after many years of blameless service he had so far forgotten himself as to oversleep. His employer (the General) was off on a journey and for the first time in thirty-five years had had to pack his own sponge bag. In the circumstances, it would hardly have surprised anyone if the General had gone off and started World War Three. In fact, there is a strongly-supported school of thought that the General is WW3.

Let us now return to the opening meet.

Whatever else it may be, it is certainly an occasion when many raw nerve ends are exposed. Raw nerves and fresh, fit, horses are a potentially explosive combination. Most hunting households experience squalls on the morning of the opening meet. The nervous state of the followers will be as nothing compared to the state of the Master and/or huntsman. I carried the horn at twenty-one opening meets. Nothing compared with my terror at the first one, but I think that the funk was only marginally less blue at the twenty-first.

Many huntsmen will have trouble sleeping through the night before the opening night. When they do drop off, their repose will be troubled by confused and nameless phantasmagoria: red, white and blue foxes who suddenly transmogrify into the hunt chairman; huge nightmares that are galloping over hounds. Your man will wake red-eyed and stale of mouth with an ever-tightening knot in his gut.

He will pick at his breakfast.

There will be interfamilial strife and bitter words will be said.

There will be frantic last-minute polishing and many frantic bleats all beginning: "Where's my . . . ?"

The loo will receive much unexpected business.

The best coat will feel too tight.

The new boots will pinch.

The good hat will clamp like a vice on the forehead.

The best horse, who is normally a paragon of virtue and who is a veteran of many opening meets, will be infected by the electricity in the atmosphere and will prance and snort and very likely give a couple of very unsettling bucks just as the huntsman is getting settled in the saddle. Mind you, I have to tell you that it used to take three men to get me on a horse: two to leg me up and one to stop me falling off the other side.

At the meet you will very likely see the hunt staff and the hounds all huddled up in some remote corner, and the reason for this unsociable behaviour is because they are terrified. They are also frightened that one of their beloved hounds will be kicked, trampled, bitten or otherwise mangled by one of the snorting, stamping, rolling-eyed, sweating creatures who are milling about outside the exclusion zone.

There are many reasons for a Master/huntsman to feel nervous at the opening meet. For the duration of the cubhunting season, he has been doing his own thing and pursuing the even tenor of his ways with no thought for anyone except his hounds. All this changes with the opening of the season proper. The huntsman now has to get his finger out and show sport for the assembled multitudes; not just at the opening meet but on all the hunting days thereafter. He it is who will have to go first across the country, with no one to "soften" the fences for him.

From the moment he gets on his horse in the morning until the moment he slides wearily off it at night he will have to concentrate 150 percent, with several different kinds of data being input and processed at the same time. He has to process the hounds and what they are doing, the movements (or the likely movements) of the fox; the likes and dislikes of all the farmers whose land he is likely to cross; the weather; the actions of the followers. He has to think ahead, behind, and both sides at once. Sit a moment and think about it and you will then have some inkling as to why Masters and huntsmen are sometimes just a little short on humour. It is a miracle that they manage to retain any at all.

Another problem with opening meets is that they happen at Traditional Venues. Jolly good, I hear you say, all for keeping up tradition. Tradition and its maintenance is the reason why the Blankshire Hounds still have their opening meet at Prodnose Hall, the home of the Prodnose (pronounced Prose) family since the first acorn. Many generations of Prodnoses have been masters of the Blankshire and many generations of opening meets have been held in front of the ancient house with its gracious parkland setting. What better place for a traditional occasion, you may ask? Yes, but times change.

While the incumbent Prodnose spends most of his time frolicking with his friends on some Greek island, the house is currently let to the County Council as a refuge for Derelict Driving Instructors; the shooting is let to a Multinational who uses it for corporate entertaining and the headkeeper is a notorious vulpicide. Nether Snidley, which used to be the estate village, is now an Urban Resettlement Area. The other side of the park is neatly enclosed by the M6040 — Skegness to Bodmin Motorway. All in all, you can see that Prodnose Hall is no longer the choicest place to go hunting, but just you try suggesting a change: you will think that the sky fell on you. It is tradition, you see.

Let us talk about hunting a pack of hounds. It is quite obvious that not all Backwoodsmen get to hunt hounds. Backwoodsmen may be an endangered species, but they are not so thin on the ground that there are enough packs of hounds to go round. It is, however, an accepted fact that every Backwoodsman's grandfather hunted hounds: that, at least, is what they will all tell you.

The other side of the coin is that nearly all the people who do hunt hounds are Backwoods-bred. The qualities that make a successful huntsman are mostly innate and are absorbed from the country as a tree absorbs sap.

These days it is fashionable to ignore the effects of breeding and heredity in human beings. You do so at your peril. No one who wishes to breed animals successfully would dream of ignoring the importance of bloodlines and pedigrees. A human is only an animal, albeit supposedly a superior one. In my opinion, there are some humans who should on no account be bred from. There is a saying that such and such a family has "a bad drop (of blood) in it". That bad drop, or inherited characteristic, is bound to come out; it might miss a generation, or even two, but surface it will. If you have studied the pedigrees you will at least be expecting it.

The inherited characteristic that every huntsman has to have is "dogginess". There are certain people with whom dogs have an instinctive empathy: it is a gift from God, like "hands" for a horseman.

No one can hunt a pack of hounds unless they are a "dog man". It matters not how hard they try, nor how much time, care and affection they lavish on their hounds — they will never really win them.

The dog man will weave "the thread". The thread is hunting patois for the empathy that connects the mind of the dog man to his dogs. You see it with collie dogs and gun dogs, but its most amazing manifestation is with a huntsman whose mind is wired into the mind of not just one hound, but all his hounds.

There are two situations which I think best demonstrate this control system.

The first is the woman walking her dog (I expect the problem could arise with a man walking his dog, but it is always women I have met). For some reason, which I know not, very few women are doggy. Many is the time that I have been walking along with, perhaps, forty couples of hounds, and I have met a Lady with her Cur Dog (note: all dogs that are not Hounds are Cur Dogs; yea, verily, even unto Crufts Champions). All Cur Dogs hate Hounds, whom they recognise as superior beings; they rage at them, rush round them and shriek hysterical abuse. The behaviour of the dog is as nothing to the behaviour of the owner who will flap about screaming

"Sit!", "Heel!" and wave an ineffectual lead. I have usually found it best to stop and wait patiently during this exhibition, otherwise one may have been pursued by the dog (and ergo its owner) for a considerable distance which would have ruined the peace of the day and run the risk of giving the poor old thing a heart attack. So I would stand and wait amongst my patient hounds until at last Poochikins allowed itself to be reclaimed and put in restraint by the owner. The immediate response of the panting and dishevelled owner would be to start abusing my hounds and me for being on the road and upsetting her poor little diddums.

The only possible response to that was to raise the hat and continue on the even tenor of one's way; reflecting, perhaps, on my father's dictum that "patience is a virtue possessed by few men, and no women".

The other prime example of the thread is at a check, out hunting. This is the moment when hounds have been hunting a fox (or whatever their quarry may be) and are for some reason at fault. The immediate response of some huntsmen to this is to start galloping madly about, shouting and trumpeting. You may hear these loons referred to as "quick huntsmen". This means that they lose foxes quickly and their hounds will soon withdraw their co-operation from such clowns.

The dog man is apparently doing nothing and you may hear references to his "slowness", but if you watch carefully you will observe that he is able to move his hounds just by moving his horse, remaining in silence himself. The thread is working. By the thread, the dog man can move his hounds like you can move the cursor on a computer monitor.

How is it done? If you are a dog man, you will not have to ask that question; if you are not, then there is no point in trying to explain it to you.

Perhaps you are wondering why I am banging on about all this. In as much as there is an autobiographical element in this book, then you have to understand that for some thirty years hunting a pack of hounds was my whole life.

I went to a school that had its own pack of beagles (that great Backwoodsmens' borstal near Slough). I was not a success at school and the only thing I brought away from it was a love of hounds and a stubborn determination to hunt a pack one day. I achieved this ambition at the ripe age of twenty-three, but I have to tell you that it was a hard, cold road getting there. Even when I did achieve the eminence I sought, it often seemed as though the wind was always blowing in my face. Hunting can be a cruel and demanding mistress, raising you to the heights of ecstasy one day and grinding you into misery the next. However, I stayed the course until 1987 against what often seemed considerable odds.

I held on for two reasons.

The first reason is that I was very good at hunting hounds; hounds worked their butts off for me, and vice versa. I do not apologise for this seeming immodesty because I happen to believe that it is the truth. I will even supply you with a reference. I have hugged this remark to my chest for years, but now that I am retired and getting fatter and smellier, I am prepared to share it with you. I was judging a puppy show with a famous professional huntsman. We were chatting between classes and he said that he understood that I was good enough to have been a professional huntsman: stand on me, that was not a lightly-awarded accolade.

The other reason that I survived is that I loved hounds and hunting with an intensity which made it possible to survive and overcome difficulties, disappointments, discomforts, disasters, and humiliation; all of which came my way.

There were years of poverty and squalor. Years of coming in wet and chilled to the bone: too tired to eat, let alone cook a meal. Years of starting at six in the morning and to be still skinning stinking sheep at one o'clock the following morning.

Years of going hunting rotten with influenza or semi-crippled from the last day's fall. Years of being verbally abused by Hunt Committees, slandered by people whose sport I was subsidising, and accepting the abuse of angry farmers.

It was all part of the job and all worth it because of the other times, the other side of the coin.

The pleasure and satisfaction of being adored by a pack of hounds.

The friendship and kindness received from country people in all walks of life — friendships which survive and remain with me.

Memories of much laughter, and of the doors that only foxhunting has opened for me.

The glory of the English countryside: its sights, its smells, its sounds, its seasons, and the privilege to see parts of it which are secret from the majority of folk.

Most of all, the Hunting.

The sight of a fox: there is no more beautiful or graceful animal in Britain. I love to see a fox at any time and will watch cubs playing for hours when I should be doing something else. I would never dream of killing a fox except on a hunting day, but then I would pursue him relentlessly and want my hounds to catch him more than anything else in the world at that moment. All good huntsmen have this attitude and it is what makes a good pack of hounds — a good huntsman will all the time be gnashing his teeth and thinking "Fox! Fox!"; his hounds will know what he is thinking and will also be gnashing their teeth and thinking "Fox! Fox!": it is the "varmintyness", the "venom" that all good huntsman/hound combinations have.

You may find this impossible to understand. You cannot conceive how a reasonably rational and fairly intelligent human being can love and admire an animal and yet on certain days seek to kill it. I have no doubt that you will be able to find some psychological explanation which will satisfy you. All I can tell you is that if you do not understand naturally, then you never will.

The hounds were the all important thing for me. It is not that I did not appreciate good horses when I had them. The pleasure of going fast across country on a good horse is not to be underestimated, but it was always a side dish for me. The horse was simply the most efficient means of keeping with hounds.

The hounds are the thing. That magical moment when the first hound speaks in the covert, the swelling cry, and then the sight and sound of hounds as they come pouring out over the covert fence and go swinging away in the open. The sight of hounds running and driving like a flock of gulls on a dark sweeping hillside, their cry floating back to you on the wind.

There was a certain hunt which I have always thought of as the best of all the hunts I have known. It was a hunt of four hours and the distance on paper was twenty-five miles: hounds would have covered much more. Towards the end of the hunt, hounds ran down into a deep wooded dale. Never before, or since, have I heard quite such a cry — wild — deep — triumphant: it makes my neck prickle now as I write about it. As the old men used to say: "they had blood in their voices" and within minutes they caught their fox in the river. I could still take you through every step of that hunt, but that cry was something special.

I have tried to give some inkling as to why I loved hunting hounds so much but I do not expect I have made you fully understand. It is usually a mistake to try to explain one of the soul's microchips. It would probably have been quicker and simpler if I had just said that hunting a pack of foxhounds was quite simply the most exciting and fulfilling thing that I have known, and I loved it.

That is enough soul baring for the moment. Backwoodsmen don't go in for too much self-analysis on the whole, but I hope that this book will also be read in the States, and that sort of thing goes down big over there with the Cousins, so you may expect a bit of it from time to time.

Let us now look at some of the more general aspects of hunting.

Let us start with Falls. I am sure that most people would agree with Mr Jorrocks that "a fall is a hawful thing". Everybody who goes hunting has falls and Backwoodsmen are no exception to that rule. Indeed, many of them are very "hard men to hounds", which does not mean that they are unkind to dogs, it means that they go across country like the proverbial manure off a shovel and break lots of things (including themselves) in the process.

I have had all sorts and conditions of falls. It is a particularly sick-making moment, that split second in time when you realise that the partnership of horse and rider is about to be dissolved and that there is absolutely nothing that you can do about it. It is an even nastier moment when you realise that your erstwhile partner is going to roll on you.

I have been rolled on, jumped on, dropped in ditches (both dry and wet), catapulted head first into a blackthorn hedge and left swimming in the River Dart on a bitter January day.

There was a famous occasion when I was sitting sulking in a Somerset rhyne (a few feet of stagnant water and bottomless primeval ooze) with not much of me showing. The whole pageant of the chase, including my hounds and my horse, had swept by and left me to contemplate my immediate future.

Two farmers came riding by. Said one: "There's a nice 'unting 'at floating there, Garge; I'll 'ave 'ee." The cap was removed from my head. "Cor bugger, look: the Master's underneath 'un."

"Well, put the Bugger's hat back and leave 'un bide quiet then. 'Tis the best place for 'un, I reckon," with which my hat was replaced and I carried on sulking.

The great thing to remember about falls out hunting is that you must not expect any sympathy for your plight.

A certain northern hunt was going hard when they were confronted with a very large stone dyke (wall). The wife and daughter of the owner of the wall were out hunting and good manners dictated that everyone should pause and politely suggest to the senior lady that as it was her wall she should have first crack (and we use the word advisedly) at it. This she very gallantly did.

It is not unusual, should your horse hit a dry stone wall hard enough, for part of the wall to collapse. It may also happen that you and your horse may also collapse. It is then possible that the horse will get up and gallop away, leaving you upside down in a pile of stone feebly waving your legs in the air.

All these things happened to our intrepid Matron and the rest of the followers who had been interested spectators suggested to the daughter that she should see how her mother was; after all, hounds were running hard and their cry was getting fainter by the minute.

The dewy eyed nymphette obligingly rode up to the legs and said, "Hey Mam, shift yer bum. There's a whole flap of folk waiting to jump there."

In all my years of falling and funking, and slipping through gates on every possible opportunity, I have only once been found guilty of performing an undoubted equestrian feat.

It happened thus.

I was having a day with a pack of hounds that was not mine own. I had been lent a horse by a dealer friend of mine whose actions may not have been entirely altruistic. It was a very good horse. The dealer described it as a "keen ride". Those of you who know Dealerspeak will know that that meant that it pulled like the proverbial train. Those of you who know dealers further will not be surprised to hear that the horse had a plain snaffle (bad brakes) in its mouth and a pair of leather reins about as thick as a boot lace. I should also mention that it was a pouring wet day. In case you do not know what rain does to leather, I will tell you that it makes leather very slippery. To equate the situation in motoring terms, it was like driving a fast car with the accelerator jammed, no brakes and limited steering.

It was in this happy situation that I found myself being carried (very neatly) over a fence and into a field of winter corn. As you may know, one does not ride across winter corn. One is expected to proceed in an orderly manner and single file around the edge of the field and debouch through a convenient gateway.

My horse was having none of this namby-pamby nonsense. He could hear hounds running and his motto was "Be with them I will".

Thus, we set off across the winter corn. I was dimly aware of people shouting at me but there was little or nothing that I could do to ameliorate the situation.

At the end of the field was a fence. Further up the same fence the followers were filing politely through a gate.

There were to be no gates for us, my steed and I. He saw the fence and (good horse that he was) cocked his ears and went for it. He was a superb jumper which was just as well.

It is my instinct when jumping a strange fence to look down and see what jollities may be in store. The first thing that I noticed, as we sailed through the air, was a lady on a horse with her mouth open. Nothing extra-ordinary in that you may say, except that horse, lady and mouth were all below looking up at us.

We were hovering in the air above a sunken lane.

To this day I can remember that moment of awful realisation, and my subsequent cry to the Almighty should be regarded as a genuine plea for help rather than a blasphemous interjection. As one interested witness said afterwards: "he said Jesus Christ when he came over the fence and he had time for the entire Lord's Prayer before he landed."

There were two fortunate circumstances. Apart from the lady with the mouth, all the other riders were grouped further up the lane, so that the Drop Zone was clear. The other bit of luck was that it was a green lane, not tarmac. I have said that the horse was a good one and, thank God, he was. A lesser horse might have crumpled on impact. He twisted in mid air, to accommodate the lane, and landed galloping: he never missed a beat.

My terror was so great that I remained glued to the saddle; too frightened to fall off.

About a mile down the lane, hounds had checked and the horse came to a halt naturally, ears cocked, watching the hounds. I had time to assume an air of blasé indifference before the field came thundering up.

The next day a friend and I went back with a measuring tape. The drop from the top of the fence to the bottom of the lane was twenty-two feet; add a further couple of feet for the height the horse jumped and you get . . . what you get is a very long way down; stand on me, a very long way down.

Whatever winter pastime the Backwoodsman may choose to pursue, the chances are that he will get cold and wet doing it. We must except shooters from the cold and wet. In the old days, Shooting Chappies also suffered from the weather. Modern Shooting Chappies are soft and pink and puffy. They get driven about in superheated Range Rovers (what *is* the difference between a Range Rover and a hedgehog) and at the first breath of wind or sprinkle of rain, they retire to some oven-temperatured building and refresh themselves with cordials that make them pinker and puffier than ever.

Those of us who spend a great deal of our working and pleasuring life out in the depths of the Backwoods do get very wet and very cold.

Hunting in particular can be very uncomfortable. I remember one day when the sky was weeping that particularly nasty brand of cold, seeping rain which only the North Sea can produce: a rain that relentlessly seeps through every layer of clothing and into every nook and cranny of the body and thence into the very marrow of the bones, where it starts to crumble your very soul.

On such a day we had conducted a fruitless quest for a fox. Foxes are not bloody fools. They do not come out to play on days like that. They stay at home and watch the racing on the telly, I should not wonder.

On such a day we progressed gloomily through the countryside until the voice of sense and reason made itself heard. It was a small voice, as it might be the voice of a young boy: "Mam, me bum's knackered. I want to go home." It was about the only sensible thing that anyone had said all day. So that was what we did.

Most of my memories of intense discomfort concern coming home from hunting. In this respect modern conditions are an improvement. These days hounds and horses go everywhere on wheels and I am all in favour. It is a good moment when hounds are curled up in their straw and the berugged horses are tucking into their hay nets in the back of the lorry. The Backwoodsman can then ease himself out of his sodden coat and heave on the great heavy overcoat that belong to his grandfather. He can then clamber into the cab of the lorry, get the heater going and look forward to that first delicious sip of hot tea from the thermos. It is a good moment.

December

So what happens in the Backwoods in December? Not a lot really. There is liable to be a nip of frost in the air and I will need gloves for riding Rupert about the farm. Rupert, you see, has to earn his keep as a tractor as well as enjoying his moments of glory in the hunting field.

We have discussed the many problems of feeding concentrates to ewes. I do that in the morning. At this time of year, the ewes get hay as well and that is my afternoon job and I rather look forward to it. I drive Rupert in beside the stack of bales in the shed and load the trailer. Set out around the fields are clusters of hay hecks (racks). The hecks have little metal wheels and each day they are moved onto a bit of clean and unpoached ground — or they should be. Sometimes they are frozen into the ground and require a hefty shoulder shove to get them moving.

Open the lid, put the bale in the rack, cut the strings and spread out the folds of hay. This is a moment I relish because if the hay was well made, well baled and well got, then each bale is a time capsule. As you open up the bale, there is a momentary whiff of the scents of summer that have been trapped in the bale and now fleet across the nostrils, and disappear.

It is a moment to savour, but not for long. The hands have been ungloved to open the knife and the deepening frost fastens on the fingers and — damn, where on earth did I put the knife? ****/£$% and &/$£: I had it in my hand to cut the strings, put it down somewhere to spread the bale and now it has disappeared. I am always doing this. The English countryside is covered with a steel carpet of pocket knives that I have put down somewhere and never found again. I thought I had once solved this problem. I bought a special knife for cutting the string of bales: it had a bright orange handle so that it would show up when you laid it down and a thong to dangle it from your wrist so that you did not have to. It was an absolutely splendid idea — until I laid it down some-where one day and . . .

Ah! there is the knife; I had stuck it into the next bale — so that I would have no trouble finding it again. The ewes quickly cluster round the newly-filled heck and I go on to the next one.

As the red sun sinks slowly in the west, the closing credits scroll down the screen, the collies jump up on the now empty trailer and we all trundle majestically home for a cup of tea.

Not a dry eye in the house.

As it is December, let us think about Goats. Now it is possible that you may think that goats are not very Backwoodsmanly creatures. You may associate goats more with earnest men in sandals and Earth Mothers with hairy legs. Your associations are your own problems, but I would agree with you that, by and large, taking the broad view and having regard to all the relevant facts, the number of goat-loving Backwoodsmen is not large. I do not think that the tale that I am about to unfold is likely to add to the sum total of goat fanciers in the Backwoods and I do hope that you are not going to say something at this stage that you will regret later: we all know the story about the chap in the Barsetshire Fusiliers, but I would point out that that was a sheep. We are talking about goats. Why are we talking about goats in December? Because what I am about to tell you happened in December.

I was driving home from hunting one evening in a relaxed and benevolent frame of mind. I was coming down by Ebbie Vincent's place and I saw that the yard light was on and that my chum Harold's car was parked in the yard.

How nice, I thought, Ebbie must be having a tea party, and decided to join it.

In fact, what I walked into seemed more like a wake than a tea party.

Ebbie had a problem.

Ebbie had bought some lambs from a far-off friend. The Far-Off Friend had undertaken to deliver them and, in return, had requested a favour of Ebbie. The FOF was a dealer and amongst his commodities for dealing were goats which were then coming into favour as producers of fine wool. The FOF had an Angora billy goat that was due to be delivered to an address quite close to Ebbie, but rather out of the way for the FOF who was always in a hurry; could he leave billy with Ebbie when he delivered the lambs and could Ebbie just pop it down the road at his leisure? No problem.

The lambs arrived and last (but far from being least) the FOF's lady friend came out of the lorry leading the billy: a vast, barbated and odiferous creature with a magnificent set of horns above a cynical and wicked-looking face. In spite of its formidable appearance, the goat trotted quietly out behind the lady friend and was led into a pen.

Just one small thing to point out, said the FOF, as he put his lorry into gear, just one small matter concerning the billy: the billy was as sweet and gentle as could be with a woman, but could be just a little bit difficult with members of the male sex.

Ebbie was able to prove this next morning when he ventured into the goat's pen and came out in one piece only by doing a very fair impersonation of an Intercontinental Ballistic Missile. The billy made it very plain that it was not a supporter of glasnost.

However, this seemed to be only a minor setback. The

goat was a transient and it was only a matter of getting Mrs Ebbie to load the billy into the farm truck and away down the road.

Mrs Ebbie is a lady both physically imposing and temperamentally mercurial. She and Ebbie discussed the matter whilst he was bent over the kitchen table having his goat-damaged tail fins comprehensively iodined.

In spite of full and frank discussions and a full review of all the relevant facts, the Vincents failed to reach agreement in this matter. Mrs Ebbie wanted nothing to do with the goat and Ebbie was not exactly in the best position to pursue the argument with any great conviction. Anyway, they came to words and Mrs Ebbie departed in high dudgeon and the family car with the avowed intention of staying with her mother until the farm had been comprehensively degoated.

Thus was Ebbie left with a problem and it was at this time that Harold and I descended upon him in search of tea.

It was quite obvious, once we had heard the enormity of the problem, that no solution would be forthcoming out of a mere tea cup: it was a whisky-and-fruit-cake problem if ever there was one and, anyway, Ebbie did not know where the tea pot was.

It required the consumption of quite a lot of fruit cake before we had the problem roped and on the floor. It was really quite simple.

All we had to do was to find a woman to lead the goat.

But we had no woman.

Let us find a woman.

But where were we to find a woman at this time of night (we had eaten a lot of fruit cake and that takes time) and even if we did find one, how would she react to a suggestion that she come and lead a goat about? Women are so inclined to misinterpret the most innocent male suggestions.

Another piece of cake was called for.

"Ahha!" said Harold. "Let us create a woman."

We thought about this biblical proposition for a bit and both Ebbie and I put our fingers on the nub of the problem: "How?" we said.

"Simple," said Harold and it was. One of us would put on one of Mrs Ebbie's dresses and become instantly female and irresistible to the crosser sort of billy goat.

The only question was who would best fill the part?

"Good heavens," I cried, "why are you blighters looking at me?"

"Because," they said licking their lips, "you are the only one big enough to fill one of Marina's (such was the lady's name) dresses."

I resolutely refused to take off my boots and breeches and so it was decided that the good lady's ball gown might be the best answer as it would hide everything.

What, I wondered, about my moustache and stubble?

The other two regarded this as a purely frivolous objection. This was the age of the Liberated Woman, they pointed out: lots of women had copious amounts of facial hair and probably smelled just as bad as I did and, anyway, they could tip a bit of this scented talcum powder down the front of my breeches.

I suppose that you get better at getting into a ball gown with practice and I think we would have got on quicker had we appreciated that you get into it from underneath (I think) and, anyway, you get on better if you take your spurs off first. I am sure that you know all these things, but I am just pointing them out as I go along. Anyway, the whole process is very wearing and entails a lot of tugging and pulling and funny little hooks that either will not do up or tear off if you breathe. I do not know how you girls dance in the wretched things.

Big though Mrs Ebbie is, it was still a considerable problem to persuade her dress about me. There were some sinister tearing noises and the back refused to do up at all. It was something of a snug fit but, if I say it as should not, I thought that I looked very fetching as I twirled in front of the looking-glass be-tulled and sequinned with the sweetest little lace collar.

I am not sure that my disguise would have fooled many people but the billy goat thought that I was the best thing since Betty Grable. He positively simpered when he saw me and allowed himself to be led out and ensconced in the back of my car without the slightest objection.

Ebbie and Harold waved us a fond farewell.

The goat's destination was a farm some ten miles down the main road.

For the first mile or two, I was buoyed up by the heady effects of fruit cake and a certain sense of novelty and adventure. This euphoria quickly came to be replaced by a certain sense of malaise. This malaise was caused by a number of things: fatigue, indigestion and, most of all, Odeur de Bouc.

I do not know how many of you have been in close proximity with a billy goat but, and let us not resort to facile euphemisms in this matter, the fact is that they pong a bit. No, that is incorrect; they *stink*. They stink with a rankness and a ferocity which the uninitiated can only guess at. In the close confines of a car, they soon make their presence felt.

Worse was to come.

The billy obviously considered that I really was the Buttered Bun. It began to nuzzle my neck and its BO was reinforced by full strength, force nine, halitosis.

"Gerroff!"

"Maaaaa!"

In spite of the cold winter night and my somewhat scanty attire, I opened the window full, allowing in a blast of cold air. This somewhat alleviated the smell, but it seemed to give the goat an appetite. It began to nibble my lovely lace collar.

I scrabbed frantically with my left hand in the well behind my seat and, hoorah, found the jack handle.

I tried to swipe the Billy about the head with some back-handed thrusts, but the billy obviously interpreted this as a mark of endearment.

I have the greatest possible respect for our constabulary. I feel that they have a hard and often thankless row to hoe. I think I can imagine how boring it must be sitting in your jam butty car on some lonely road on a cold winter's night, yawning, bored out of your skull and waiting for something to happen: as it might be "a vehicle proceeding in an erratic manner." The obvious course of duty is then to stop the offending vehicle with flashing lights and lots of klaxon (gets the old adrenalin pumping). You then don your cap in the approved fashion, approach the vehicle in a stately manner and bend down to address the occupant.

It is just possible that you may be mildly surprised to find that the car is apparently being driven by a moustached transvestite who has been to a ball (if you will pardon the expression), but your experience over the years in the Gendarmerie has probably hardened you to most manifestations of human weakness.

What no experience has prepared you for is a wicked-looking horned and bearded head that suddenly appears over the driver's shoulder, belches comprehensively, and foully, in your face and then removes the aforementioned uniform cap and begins to eat it.

I mentioned at the beginning of the goat saga that it all began as I was driving home from hunting one evening. But in the old days hounds and horses travelled on their own feet to the meet, hunted, and shambled home again. This could make for a long day.

As a very young man, I whipped-in to a pack of hounds who had no transport. Our farthest meet was over twenty miles from the kennels, which meant a four- or five-hour hack at each end of the day. I can still remember the weary ache of those rides home in the dark, often wet through and chilled, and always weary. I used to doze off in the saddle, which is not recommended procedure, and when one got home at nine, ten, eleven o'clock at night, hounds and horses were to "do" before we got sip, sup or flash of firelight.

Hacking home is even less fun if you are lost.

A certain man went hunting in a strange country. The dimpsey (twilight) found him alone on a stretch of dreary moor. I need hardly add that it was raining, the fog was down on the hill tops, his horse had lost a shoe and he had not the slightest clue as to where he might be.

At last he found a sort of track which led him to some

sign of civilisation in as much as it ran alongside a barbed wire fence on the other side of which was a concurrent bog. A gap in the cloud wrack revealed a hill top beyond the bog. On the hill top was a man leaning on a stick, a collie dog at his feet. The traveller grasped at this ray of hope.

There was no way, however, that he could approach the hill by horse, so he tied his horse to the fence, tore his breeches climbing over it, fell up to his waist in a bog hole, and then had to struggle uphill through a zariba of thorn and gorse.

At last he arrived, panting, dishevelled and squelching at the top of the hill.

The man leaning on the stick regarded him with gloomy, soggy interest.

The collie bit him.

The wretched traveller begged to be put on the right road to Muxworthy (yes, you are quite right: Devon).

The farmer removed his dripping hat and scratched his head. He had lived round yere all his born days and he'd never yeard tell of Muxworthy.

The traveller thanked him through gritted teeth and set off down through the thorns and the bog, over the manhood-endangering barbed wire fence and back to his trusty steed. He was just untying the reins when down the wind came distant shouting.

The traveller lifted up his eyes unto the hill. On the cloudy top he could now dimly make out two figures with assorted dogs. Both men were waving their hats and shouting. It seemed obvious that intelligent reinforcements had arrived, bursting with information about Muxworthy.

Once more the traveller bestrode the wire.

Once more he squelched and floundered through the bog.

Once more he made a frontal assault on the rugged slope and carried the summit in spite of the harassing tactics of the massed collie dogs.

There were indeed two old men leaning on their sticks and watching his arrival with dripping calm.

The first old man spoke: "This yere's my neighbour. 'E've lived yere all 'is life an 'e've never yeard tell of Muxworthy neither."

My Birthday happens in December.

Backwoodsmen tend to be big on birthdays. Your *average* Run-of-the-Mill Backwoodsman tends to be a social creature and he likes to share his joy at being another year older with his chums.

He might very well descend on London and take over the Savoy for the evening.

It is quite possible that he might erect a marquee on the lawn and invite the county in for an evening of dining, dancing to Marvin Merryman and the Marinated Musikeers (you *must* have heard of them), bread-roll throwing and general wild licence.

I will have none of this.

As a child, not only was I dragged kicking and screaming to other children's parties ("you'll enjoy it when you get there") but, horror of horrors, I was expected to welcome all the little bleeders back on *my* birthday. I fear that the experience scarred me for life and I have been a total social failure ever since.

In fact I hardly mention my birthday these days just in

case somebody takes it into their head to use it as an excuse for a party. You think that that is unlikely and so do I, but you never know with party people: the thought of jelly and fairy cakes can make them most unscrupulous. A steak and kidney pie, a bottle of decent Burgundy and a cigar by my own fireside, that is my idea of a good birthday night out — or rather in.

The only time that I can remember getting lit up on my birthday was my twenty-first.

Were did I go? Dinner at the Café Royal perhaps? Party at the 400? Late-night loucheness at the Bag of Nails (all this dates me a bit)? Well, no; I was pretty skint in those days and living fairly basically in a caravan. I am afraid that the Savoy was out, fond though I have become of that splendid place. No, Old Jack organised my birthday party.

It may be that some amongst you are unfamiliar with the works of R. S. Surtees. Surtees is a supreme Backwoodsmanly author and if you have missed out on him so far, then you have denied yourself much pleasure. Anyway, those of you who have read Surtees would instantly recognise Old Jack.

Jack was a large and prosperous Wessex Yeoman. He always claimed to have started farming with a cow, a donkey and an acre of land; when I knew him he was farming some 1,500 acres.

Jack and I used to go on the toot occasionally. He used to drive one of those big old Rovers, always with the handbrake half on. "I likes to keep her curb chain good and tight; then the bugger can't get away with me."

Jack also kept his own rather motley pack of beagles, which by virtue of the fact that he always (very sensibly) hunted them on a horse, were known as the Hollybower Harriers.

"Now Little Willy," he said, "you come down along of us for your birthday. Us'll have a beef steak pudden made down at the pub. He can stop the night here, can't 'ee, Mother? And you can hunt my hounds for your birthday present. Now then?" That was an offer I could not refuse.

I must be honest and say that I cannot remember too much of the evening. I do remember the beefsteak pudding for which the lady of the pub was justly famous, with that lovely crisp suet crust that you broke through to get to all the goodies within. In fact, I have to tell you that the only place that I have eaten a beefsteak pudding that was anywhere comparable was at the Savoy.

I do remember that the assembled company presented me with a very nice briar pipe which gave me great pleasure for many years.

I also remember Jack reciting a poem which began:
"Here we suffer grief and pain,
Over the road, they're just the same . . ."
but I'm sorry to say that the remainder of the evening is obscured by mists which can only be those of time; all except for the journey home.

The journey from the pub to Manor Farm is neither long nor arduous: five minutes of a walk.

Walking was not high on my list of priorities by the end of the evening. The assembled company brought to bear on this problem the gravitas that is only induced by a considerable intake of beefsteak pudding. The considered opinion of the gathering was that the pub wheelbarrow was the answer to the problem and into this fine old-fashioned wooden conveyance I was eventually placed. The next problem was: who was going to push the barrow?

There was considerable disagreement as to whom this honour should fall and at last it was decided by a good old British compromise: everyone would get a turn at pushing the barrow and its comatose cargo. It would be propelled in shifts: two men at a time.

There is one undeniable fact about wheelbarrows: they were never designed to be driven by a committee; it simply does not work. What happens is that the man on the right handle pushes harder than the man on the left, or stops without warning to attend to nature, or a fierce argument breaks out about almost anything from the Theory of Relativity to Store Lamb Prices. Whatever, the one certainty in all this is that the barrow is going to tip over and its load is going to be spread in road or ditch.

After about the fourth of these upsets, I came to somewhat groggily and announced my intention of walking the rest of the way.

The assembled company entered a firm *nolle prosequi* (*nem con*): how were they all to get a turn unless I remained in the barrow? Fair play for all was the cry: the greatest good for the greatest number and if that meant a little wear and tear on my person, well then tough titty on me.

I cannot honestly say that being continuously tipped out of a wheelbarrow is the best way of sobering up a chap, but I do seem to remember it being remarkably successful. It certainly made a big impression (well, several actually) on me at the time. The memory lingers on.

But it was a happy birthday.

Perhaps one of the reasons that I do not enjoy my birthday as I might is that I am depressed by the imminence of Christmas which falls a week later.

I have a deep-seated aversion to Christmas: I think that there are two reasons for this.

The first reason is that I was frightened by Father Christmas at an impressionable age. I was brought from my room to the family gathering and told to expect a big surprise. Sure enough there he was, Father Christmas himself: red suit, hood, white bushy beard, the lot. Santa was just winding himself up for his first "Ho Ho Ho" when I fled screaming from the room and went and buried myself under my pillow. Now, of course, you know, and I now know, that it was only the butler dressed up for the occasion; the real Santa had a lame reindeer and was delayed somewhere over Narvik. However, it is another of those lasting impressions and may well account for my somewhat hesitant approach to Christmas.

The second reason for my dislike of Yuletide is misanthropy. I suppose that if I were into psycho babble and/or lived in Hampstead, I would say that I was an immensely *private* person and just needed some space to get myself together. That is a load of horse manure. I just do not like people very much and I especially do not like them when they hold jollity rallies in my armchair.

You see Christmas is all about the Family.

Backwoodsmen are big on Family Christmasses. They like to amass as many generations as possible about them, even unto the remotest degrees of Cousincy. It is my belief that most cousins benefit from being remote: Australia perhaps.

Mrs Poole is very strong on the Family Christmas. Our snug little house groans at the seams, I just do not know where she finds them all. In fact, my wife's family are a source of despair to me. I just think that I have got the family tree in some sort of order when, Hey Presto! she conjures up another relation like a rabbit from a hat.

My armchair, which is normally strictly reserved for my particular backwoodly bottom, is suddenly permanently occupied by second cousins twice removed. It is only the strength of the wife's personality that prevents them from being removed yet a third time; forcibly.

My brother and sister-in-law come to stay. I am devoted to them both, but there are essential differences between my brother and me: he is a p.m. person and I am an a.m. person. I like to rise early and go early to bed, my brother likes to rise at midday, rubbing his hands at the prospect of twelve hours' relentless fun and festive mirth from which there will be no remission for good conduct.

Every way I turn, I am besieged by junior relations, liberally smeared with chocolate, who regard me as something ideal for wiping their hands and faces on. No, no, of course I didn't hit the child, I just rearranged its ear a bit; well, it is only slightly bent. *I am not shouting.*

The pressure is unremitting. There is a three-line whip on jollity. At every minute of the day there is someone trying to force me into a paper hat and someone else exhorting me to "cheer up; its Christmas".

I sometimes think that the best Christmas I spent was my first as an MFH.

What was that, Aunt Madge? Your gall bladder? Really,

as big as that? Well, I never. The surgeon said that himself, did he? In all his long career, eh? Well I never. Gosh, how absolutely riveting.

Now, where was I ? Ah yes; the best Christmas, yes.

I was unmarried then and far from my family.

The rest of my small hunt staff were all family men, so I gave them the day off and, you will hardly believe this, five farmers rang up with dead cows they wanted shifting away from their festivities. The reason for this was quite simple. The Dog Meat man whom they would normally have rung up instead of me (ten shillings being the reason for the preference) had climbed out of his skull on Christmas Eve and was liable to spend the next forty-eight hours groaning into his pillow.

So I spent most of Christmas day on the road with the knacker truck winching in huge South Devon cows. It seemed a good way to spend the day although of course I pretended to be miserable and deprived. After I had had my bit of bread and cheese for lunch, I went in and sat with the hounds and they all told me that I was their Father Christmas.

You know, I think that child is about to be sick. Yes, I thought so. Never mind, Aunt Madge, I am sure it will wash out. Well, what was I supposed to do about it? It's got a mother, hasn't it?

If you blow that squeaker at me once more . . .

The comforting thought is that sometime during the long long afternoon I am going to have to go and give the sheep their hay. Then the collies and I can sit on the trailer and watch the wintry sun set over the Cheviots. The one thing we do do rather well round here is a spectacular sunset. Sunset over the Cheviots, whether it be winter or summer, is always worthy of a pause. I can light a pipe of peace and contentment and wonder whether they have managed to get that squeaker thing out of the Second Cousin Twice Removed's left nostril yet.

Old Year's Night is another kettle of fish. You may prefer to call it New Year's Eve, but up here in the Borders it is Old Year's Night and is quite enough trouble as it is without inventing fancy new names for it.

Seeing the Old Year off and ushering the New Year tenderly in is a serious business in this part of the world. There will be parties. The hill farms will keep open house and everyone will range from one to another. There will be some people who will spend two or three days crossing every threshold except their own.

There will be singing, dancing, not much sleeping and not a little drinking.

If the night be frosty and still and if you pause a while on the valley road, you can see the various houses with all their lights ablaze and very possibly you might hear the sounds of distant revelry on the still air. But it is too cold to stand about for long. Better to set off again to the next place of call and force yet another glass of whisky through gritted teeth.

"Howway y'auld hewer! Ye'll gie us a bit song then?"

"Way man, divn't get him singing; it's like an auld yow blaring."

"Just a bit dram, man; noo, shak hands and all the best to yee."

"Noo, wheer's yon Geordie with the accordion?"

"Arl the best, lad."

Arl the best . . . Arl the best . . . Arl the best. That is the great cry at the beginning of the year and it has to have a handshake with it.

"Arl the best" is not quite how you would describe the fettle at the New Year's Morning meet of the hounds at the Dandelion and Burdock. In fact, it would be pretty fair to say that most of the assembled company look more than a little part worn: tatty is a word that springs to mind and some of the faces look, well, lived in.

The bar of the Dandelion and Burdock has something of the air of a casualty clearing station. You might well be forgiven for the suspicion that some of those propped up in corners have the appearance of people left over from the day before. Nor should you be overly surprised to find the same firms on the same pitches that evening.

However, now is the moment for a restoring Percy Special to lubricate the works and get things moving again. It may be that there are those of you who have never experienced the beneficial effects of a Percy Special.

The Percy Special is popularly supposed to have been invented by that great man, the 10th Duke of Northumberland. It is especially designed to combat the effects of the bitter northern winter weather, to kill the worms from last night, and to generally induce a feeling of well being and good heartedness.

The Percy Special is 50 percent cherry brandy and 50 percent whisky.

A Percy Special is an alcoholic mugging.

So having staggered from December into the grey morning of New Year's Day, let us raise our Percy Specials to the beginning of a new month and a New Year.

Good Luck and Arl the Best.

January

So what does a Backwoodsman do in January? Expects bad weather if he has got any sense. Snow tends to be a feature of most Januaries, especially in the bleak Border country. In fact if I had to vote for the month that I like least then it would probably be January. It can be a month of siege and anyone who has not prepared for this may learn a sour lesson. If the wind gets set into a south-easterly direction then trouble can be expected.

The S.E. wind comes all the way from the Urals by way of the North Sea and its temper does not improve on the way.

Many people have asked me why I built my house on the west side of the wood. It must be very windy, they say, sniffing disapprovingly. So indeed it can be. But there is no such thing as having a view without having the wind and my view is worth a few windy days. Anyway, it is a west wind that we get. The west wind is basically a good-hearted benign sort of chap: big, bluff and occasionally rather over boisterous. If he were human he would tend to get rather pissed and fall over things and break them whilst singing, shouting and roaring with laughter. There is no malice in the chap.

The south-east wind is quite different. He is sour, sly and treacherous; malign and vindictive. He comes with a bone-eating chill and brings cold, seeping rain. In the winter he brings the snow. All the bad snowstorms come out of the south-east and they are the ones that last.

That is why I built the house on the west side of the wood: because it baffles the sout-east wind. On a bad day there is an overcoat difference in temperature between one side of the wood and the other. We are protected from the worst of the snow, which whistles round and blocks the farm road at the bottom end of the wood. I then have to plough a way out to the road, which will itself be blocked, until such time as the county snow blower can spare the time from keeping the bus routes open. This may be a matter of days.

I always try to have the ewes snugly tucked up in the shed before the bad weather comes. There I have the hay, straw and sheep, all under one roof. On a bad day I can lean on my fork and watch the weather swirling by outside and hissing through the sitka spruce, whilst the ewes cud contentedly on a nice dry bed of thick straw. I have heard people say that it is flying in the face of nature to house sheep. It is my experience that people who talk most about nature have the fewest dealings with that little lady. My response is that if God had not meant us to put sheep in sheds then he would not have let us invent the wretched things (sheds that is; not sheep). You can go and be as natural as you like in a blizzard any time; me and the girls will stay in our shed, thank you very much.

The south-east wind does not stay for ever although it sometimes feels like it. Our prevailing airstream is westerly and eventually our old boisterous friend will come whooping up the Irish Sea, arrive shouting and rattling round the chimney pots and the snow will go.

Then there will be floods.

Floods are a ticklish business. We have a lot of fords with water running through them; they are important in this area. If you want to go from Little Rubrick to High Cokehope (which is not pronounced the way that it is spelled) you can cut off several miles by taking the ford over the river Weemish. Before you attempt to do this, it is as well to know just how deep the water is and whether the bottom has been washed out; otherwise you might just finish up becoming a hazard to shipping somewhere off the Dogger Bank.

Perhaps a cautionary tale is in order here.

Two men set forth on a journey in high hopes and a motor car and came to a ford.

It had been a time of heavy rain and the river was up.

The question was: was the water so high as to make the ford not negotiable and cause a long detour via the main road to be necessary. The men were not locals and they did not know the ford well enough to know the answer.

However, help was at hand. There was a footbridge just below the ford and leaning on the bridge rail was a bit of local colour in the shape of a small boy wearing a snotty nose and an enormous pair of wellies. The boy was accompanied by a large and malignant-looking collie dog.

Our travellers hailed the boy and asked whether, in the light of his intimate local knowledge, he would be so gracious as to inform them as to whether, in his opinion, the river was shallow enough to allow the car to cross it safely. Or, as they put it:

"Noo then, Bonny Lad, is the witter arl reet?"

The boy considered the question and as an aid to thought redistributed the snot about his face with the back of his hand. He eventually gave it as his opinion that having taken all relevant factors into account and having regard to all the information at his disposal, there was no valid reason as to why a vehicular crossing should not be attempted and why it should not meet with success. Or as he succinctly and demotically put it:

"Whey aye, nae bother."

Our travellers returned to their car and nosed out into the flood.

Fortune is a fickle jade, but there were two positive factors in what happened next.

It was fortunate that the footbridge was downstream of the ford as the girders of the bridge were the only thing that prevented the car from heading for the North Sea.

The other piece of good fortune was that the car had a sunshine roof which enabled the travellers to escape from the rapidly rising flood and scramble up onto the bridge.

You may feel that in such shocking and sodden circumstances the travellers may have felt themselves to have been the recipients of what the RAF used to call "duff gen". You may sympathise with their somewhat aggrieved feelings; you may understand, but not condone, their gut reaction which was to assuage their unhappiness by some sort of physical retaliation against the false prophet who had urged them on to disaster.

The False Prophet was still leaning on the bridge and had been an interested spectator of the watery drama. However, any advance in his direction was greeted with bared teeth and heavy growling from the collie dog.

The travellers were forced to curb their enthusiasm for mayhem and conduct a fretful inquisition from a safe distance. Why, they asked, had he so woefully misled them as to the depth of the water?

"Why," said the youth, "yon witter arnly cooms halfway oop wor ducks."

So what else does a Backwoodsman do to while away the tedium of the long dark winter evenings?

What he may well do is to get some pheasants out of the game larder, decant some port, and having donned a well dribbled-on velvet smoking jacket, summon a select band of his neighbours (also in velvet smoking jackets) to roll up and hit the place a crack.

Then will follow a comfortable evening of browsing, sluicing and gossip. The host will wave his guests good-bye in the secure knowledge that in the near future he will don the velvet and take his place at one of their tables to eat their pheasants and slurp their port.

What of the conversation on these occasions? The staples of small talk will tend to be of foxes, pheasants and farming. There may be talk of mutual Backwoods friends. By the nature of Backwoods society, most of its members know, or know of, most of the other members. They very likely were at the same school, or served in the same regiment, or the wife was at school with the sister. Backwoodsmen are very keen on pedigrees, whether of hounds, horses or other Backwoodsmen. Mention a name and they will know its ramifications. They will know that Sinnington Gainsay '76 has umpteen lines back to the famous Brecon Paragon '23. They will know instinctively that the Bertie Prosser being talked about is first cousin to Charlie Fowey (Lord Fowey to you) and that he married Nancy Bent-ffescue, who was at school with Freddie's wife Susie and whose brother was in the Hot and Heavy Hussars with Buffy, who is, of course, second cousin to . . . etc, etc.

All in all, not very highbrow stuff; not much about the meaning of life, you may think. That is your opinion and you are entitled to it. My opinion is that people are better employed getting on with their lives than agonising about what they mean. Anyway, Backwoodsmen know exactly what their lives mean and it is no damned business of yours. I mean, a chap does not sit about all day wittering about the meaning of life; he just gets on with it, what?

Then there is dancing. I hate dancing but duty drives me to attend various terpsichorean functions. Let us take, for instance, a Hunt Dance.

Hunt Dances are held throughout the winter, usually in village halls. Village halls vary in degree from something that looks like a large chicken hut to Victorian Gothic on a grand scale.

Hunt Dances are informal and tend to be robust in character, the robustness increasing with the intake of alcohol which may be not inconsiderable and why not. I do remember, however, one dance that was held in a hall owned by the Chapel which meant that all alcohol was banned and one had to get up one's enthusiasm on cups of strong tea. I have to say that people would have this eventuality in mind and as the evening wore on, the tea definitely got stronger and bore less and less relation to the original brew.

The dancing tends to be of the old-fashioned variety. Many country people are expert dancers and take it very seriously. Popular demand favours Waltzes, Quick Steps, Foxtrots and such esoteric caperings as the Military Two Step and the Veleta. I cannot do any of these things, but I can shuffle about the floor more or less in time to the music. As long as the dance is fairly sedate and my partner comely, I can just about cope.

But up in the Borders there are additional hazards: traditional dances rear their ugly head and Scottish subversion is rife. It is my opinion that Scottish Dancing is a heathen abomination. I have long suspected that John Knox's strong feelings about the fair sex may have been the result of an early exposure to the rigours of Albannach caperings. It is quite possible that as a naïve and trusting young man he was thrust, all unsuspecting, into an Eightsome Reel. If his experiences were anything like mine were then his trumpetings about the "monstrous regiment of women" may be regarded in a more sympathetic light.

Fairly soon after I came to live in the Borders, I attended a Hunt Dance. I was standing at the bar, sipping quietly and causing offence to no one, when the bandleader announced an Eightsome Reel.

Two ladies approached me. I beamed happily upon them, little suspecting the ordeal that awaited me. I was as a lamb baring my throat to the knife.

Would I not like to participate in their team for the reel?

I politely declined.

Now the ladies of the Border are extremely comely, but they also come from hardy stock and are made of wire, steel and whipcord.

One lady removed my drink from my unsuspecting hand. The other lady put an excruciatingly painful arm lock on me and suggested that I reconsider my position.

I did.

I prefer to draw a veil over the next few minutes. I still dream of it and wake up sweating and whimpering. I remember being flung like a bundle of rags from one lovely lady to the next and becoming progressively bruised and weakened in the process. At last one especially angelic creature got me with a Forearm Jab and finally flattened me with a Step Over Toe Hold . . . 9 . . . 10 . . . OUT! shouted the referee and there was rapturous applause all around. And, what is more, someone had drunk my whisky.

I still bear the scars of the encounter to this day, along with my shredded innocence, but now I have developed the cunning and the quick reactions of all small hunted creatures. I can smell an Eightsome Reel on the wind. I am off like a long dog and remain firmly locked in the Gents for the duration.

There are other dances that require strategic withdrawal to a previously prepared position. There is for instance " The Drops of Brandy ".

Those of you who were condemned to Pony Club parties in your youth will remember a thing called "Strip the Willow" where the participants form two lines and progressively dance down the line: all very folksy and charming, as I am sure you will agree, but pretty harmless. " The Drops of Brandy " is technically similar to "Strip the Willow", but is physically as similar as Pass the Parcel is to Rugby League Football.

I suppose that I weigh in at about eighteen stone. A line of muscular hill shepherds and their ladies can get quite a lot of top spin going on an eighteen-stone man. The last (the very last) time that I performed " The Drops of Brandy " I came out at the bottom of the line spinning like a Dervish and with the muzzle velocity of a six-inch shell. They had to scrape me off the wall at the end of the room (this was in someone's house) and I must say that the host was very decent about the china cabinet, especially as I understand that one or two of the picccs were of some value (when I say "pieces" I mean before they became pieces if you see what I mean).

So that is " The Drops of Brandy " off the list, and at the slightest hint of a "Gay Gordon", I am up and running for the car park like the first long dog's brother.

So taking the dancing business all in all, I tend to spit it out; all barring the Last Waltz with Mrs Poole which is a sacrifice that I make on the altar of marital harmony.

No, I think that I am much safer in the bar. But even this haven for those with two left feet has its own problems. For instance, there is the problem of the "Dreaded Phantom Hand".

The "Dreaded Phantom Hand" seems to be a particular curse of Masters of Hounds. Now I enjoy a glass of whisky; I find it does me good, lubricates the works and generally puts me in good fettle. I can calculate my ration to the nearest glass. I know full well that there is a point of no return past which common sense is very likely to temporarily evaporate and I shall very likely start singing; then it is down hill all the way even unto chaos and anarchy. So I pace myself during an evening and monitor my intake; all goes well and merrily — until "the Hand" starts.

What happens is this. There I am standing, talking to two or three about some mutually enthralling topical issue (as it might be the current prices of anthelmintics, or whose car was parked outside Rose Cottage all Thursday night), there I am chatting quietly and suddenly a hand appears over my shoulder and tips another whisky into my glass. The extraordinary thing is that the Hand appears to be totally disembodied. One turns round quickly and the throng behind is chattering happily away amongst itself, keeping their hands to themselves. Hand? what hand? what drink? and as to the ridiculous suggestion that anyone amongst the company here assembled would be so soft as to buy me a drink — why the very idea provoked laughter and ribaldry.

I turn away and start chatting again and within five minutes the Hand is there again. The manifestation continues throughout the evening with the result that instead of a modest glass of whisky and water held daintily in the paw, I finish up with a half-pint tumbler of nearly neat whisky in each hand and am well into "The Old Rustic Bridge by the Mill". Now I am quite sure that there is a perfectly rational explanation for this phenomenon, but I am not able to provide it: not with a pint of whisky in front of me anyway.

". . . Though now far awaaaay, still my thoughts fondly stray to that ooold rustic bridge by the meeeel."

Hunt Balls are a different can of worms. This is more up-market frolicking and is usually regarded as the "Great Social Event of the Hunting Season".

Hunt Balls were traditionally held in Stately Homes. This is no longer commonplace. There are fewer stately homes about and those who have managed to hang onto them are increasingly reluctant to throw wide the stately doors to the sort of people who attend Hunt Balls in these changing times. I am not talking so much about people being sick into the Ming vase: that has been going on for years. Neither do I refer to bunging bread rolls at one's friends; Backwoodsmen are great roll chuckers. Indeed I would not dream of going to a Hunt Ball without bagging Scruffy Nateley-Scures between the eyes with a well-aimed crusty wholemeal: failure to do so would spoil my appetite for breakfast.

No, the sort of thing that gets up the nose of your average, run-of-the-mill, stately home owner is retiring to his bed to find it already vigorously occupied and him not even getting offered the chance to carve a slice off for himself. He has to send the butler to cool the intruders' ardour with buckets of water, which means that he has to take himself off to the spare room where he finds . . . but, no, the whole thing causes a lot of upset and unhappiness.

Hunt Balls do still take place in private houses and the owners take the appropriate precautions, such as moving all the furniture upstairs, wiring off the stairs with barbed wire and putting the Head Keeper behind it with a shotgun and a bottle of whisky.

Nowadays Hunt Balls more usually take place in hotels or town halls.

Wherever they take place, the punters are expected to wear full fig for the occasion. A dinner jacket at the very least. At one time it used to be tail coats: hunt evening coats like a ringmaster.

I do not know whether you have ever had to force yourself into evening dress: a starched shirt front — stiff as a cuirass, from which the studs used to fly off in moments of stress (which was quite often in my case); those ghastly wing collars which meant that I was doomed to look at the ceiling all evening, and not a glimpse of a bit of decent cleavage until I had sweated the collar into a soft enough consistency so that I could bend my neck a bit. And you try dancing all trussed up like that; it was like dancing in a suit of armour. I used to have to be taken out to the car park and walked up and down in a sweat rug until I had stopped steaming.

Somewhen in the middle seventies, men of sense and gravitas invented the Hunt Dinner Jacket, which is quite simply a dinner jacket in the colours of the hunt, and oh the blissful ease of it after evening dress. They are now the norm amongst most hunting people, but I remember that the first time I went to a Hunt Ball in one (before they became general currency) I was told that the band entrance was round the back.

I am sure that I need hardly tell you that foxhunters wear red evening dress and hare hunters wear green. I know you knew but some of the others might not have your advantages. It is an important part of the ghastly tale which I am about to unfold.

Many years ago, when I was about as feckless a youth as ever I was to become, which was never really very, I attended a Hunt Ball with some other bright young sparks. Somewhere round about midnight the band stopped for a breather and, for all I know, corned beef sarnies and a cup of strong tea.

Such was the excitement that the evening had so far engendered in our youthful breasts, that it was felt that half an hour of inactivity was scarcely to be borne. A mock hunt was suggested and the suggestion received general acclaim.

One of our party was to set off and was to be hunted by a pack of "Bitches" urged on by the frantic holloaing and hornblowing of the remainder of the party. All good Hooray Henry stuff you know. At this point, it is important that you note that the quarry was a beagler (chosen for his fleetness of foot) and that he was wearing a green tail coat.

Well my dears, it was the greatest fun. We rootled and tootled all round the building and out into the car park and back. By this time the Bitches really had their hackles up and were running for blood. Our quarry had the sense to realise that he was in trouble and very sensibly went to ground in the Gents with the good ladies baying at the door.

Two of us mere males went in to bolt the Beagler who very promptly, and wisely, went out of the window. We reported this unfortunate turn of events to the Pack, but at that moment events decided to take another turn.

A senior and very important Beagler had been enjoying some quiet supper and was returning to the ballroom up the long passage which just happened to run past the Gents.

He was wearing a green tail coat.

The Bitches were not in a mood to discriminate between tail coats and what they happened to cover. With a shrill scream of *"There he is!!!"* they flung themselves on their unsuspecting victim.

I do not know whether you have ever seen twelve excited ladies removing a volubly protesting Senior Beagler's nether garments in a passage, but it is an interesting sight. In fact, it was not possible to see the victim at all: just a mass of struggling women out of which an article of clothing would occasionally be tossed.

I must say the Senior Beagler was very decent about it when we eventually beat the Bitches off and restored him to his clothes (albeit short of a few strategic buttons). We bought him lots of drinks and he made a very quick recovery from the shock.

In case you are a tiny bit shocked, I should add that the story had a happy ending. It is my firm belief that one of the ladies was so impressed by what she had seen, as it were in passing, that she found an even better way of restoring the Senior Beagler's faith in human nature before the end of the night.

★   ★   ★

I suppose that I cannot leave the subject of dances without mentioning our Barn Dance. To mention it in January is something of an anachronism, because it happens sometime in the summer; or used to. Now read on.

Hunts are always short of money because costs keep going up and most hunting people actually think that it is jolly unfair that they, personally, should have to pay for their hunting. To raise money, hunts run all sorts of functions — dances, whist drives, bring and buy, hunter trials; the list is practically endless. What happens in practice is that these functions are attended by hunt followers from the hunt concerned and from the neighbouring hunts so that the whole thing is financially incestuous. What we all want to do is to tap into the purses and pockets of the Great British Public, for whom hunting exists only on Christmas Cards.

We used to achieve this admirable aim with our Barn Dance.

Everybody in the Hunt loathed the Barn Dance for reasons which will become apparent, but it did make quite serious money.

The aim of the venture was to attract the not so gilded youth of the local towns to come and spend their money. To this end, we used to obtain the services of some up-and-coming Rock Band and a Guest Appearance from a Radio-One Moron-of-the-Moment. This brought Voysser Youff and his lady friend flocking in. They came in leather and studs and big boots. They came crested and spiked in multi hues. They came safety-pinned and pierced and enchained and painted. They came from the city and from towns A, B and C and therein lay problems.

171

For the last 400-odd years, the youth of A, B and C have yearned to squeeze each others' windpipes and, of course, if there is any windpipe squeezing going on, the Laterally Mobile from the City are not to be left out of the fun. So what we are looking at is a security problem.

For many years we contained this problem by having very large hunt supporters (of which there are not a few) as stewards. They knew the likely troublemakers and problems were mostly nipped in the bud. There was also a large contingent of Northumbria's Finest on hand; and there was, of course, the Timber Wolf. There are those who maintain that the Timber Wolf was a standard issue Police Alsatian. Whatever, it was the size of a Shetland pony, had teeth six inches long and was secured to its robust looking handler by the sort of chain a Cunarder might use for its anchor.

Everybody who knows me knows that temperamentally I am a pussy cat. I have about as much aggression as a box of paper tissues. But I am large and some people are misled enough to find my bulk impressive. So I copped for being a steward.

Most years it was an evening of dreadful noise, discomfort and skull-numbing boredom. There was usually a minor scuffle or two, but a quiet word or two usually calmed things down. If diplomacy failed, Big Kevin would take a lad under each arm and take them out to look at the stars in the night sky.

The breeding of the normal trouble could be said to be: By Drink — Out of Jealousy and was usually two young cocks sparring off.

The Night of Trouble was caused by the Fair Sex. No, that is not quite true. The trouble began with Ms Slack

Alice and Ms Dirty Ellen. Beauty is in the eye of the beholder. If spiky hair, studded nostrils and deep-fried grime is for you, then you need to look no further than these two ladies. Anyway it seemed that Ms Slack Alice had been paying undue attention to Ms Dirty Ellen's young man. Ms Ellen felt that her rights of property were in question and recorded her disapproval by digging her finger nails into Ms Alice's cheek and pulling. Soon there was a good deal of loose hair and blood flying about and the noise cut through the best efforts of the band.

At first the male escorts of the two ladies were content to cheer and jeer from the touch line. Then Big John (showing extreme courage) took a lady in each hand and separated them. They came apart with a noise rather like tearing cloth and a hideous keening.

Peace keeping is a dangerous job. Both the supporting teams of the female protagonists felt that their side had been unfairly robbed of victory and waded in to redress the wrong.

It started to get hairy.

"Arf! Arf! Arf!" The Timber Wolf appeared to have grown to the size of a small bullock and it did seem to have an awful lot of teeth.

"*ARF! ARF! ARF!*" There are times when even the most over-excited of people are open to the forces of reason. Those joined in battle obviously felt that they were being offered a feast of reason and a flow of soul. I have never actually seen people trying to get out of a door four deep before. It was an impressive sight. The Timber Wolf continued to give his views on the situation from close behind them and suddenly it was as though the fight had never been. And the Band played on.

It was a most impressive example of crowd control and

I had a very good view from underneath the table where I had established a strategic command post, the better to direct operations.

But now perhaps you understand why we all used to hate the Barn Dance.

It does not happen any more.

The next year they burned the barn down.

One of the nice things about hunting on the hills is that one does not have to spend long hours patching and repairing fences after a day's hunting.

The facts of life are that out of a field of say one hundred horses in a "riding country" only about ten percent of the horses and riders will form that true and happy partnership of skill and ability that (deceptively) seems to flit effortlessly over hedge, ditch and rail. The remaining ninety percent cross the country in declining degrees of ability from moderate to dreadful.

Only the select few attempt to go with Bertie Luce-Rayne as he cuts out the work in his faultless swallow-tail coat. Johnny Goodegrass will attract quite a following because although he is a very hard rider and will have a go at anything, his horses are not absolutely the best and he is very likely to take the stiffness out of a fence. When he has picked himself up and remounted, his respectful tail of followers will find themselves confronted with a much softer option.

If you really want the sting taken out of the fences then

you can do no better than to follow the redoubtable Sir Spurde Feele-Boote. Sir Spurde with his jolly red face and white moustache rides a generous twenty stone. His enormous horses are not always the most agile, but the team motto is "Be with them we will" and no fence is turned away from. It is an awesome sight to see a ton of horse and rider coming into a fence, secure in the knowledge that their momentum is such that what they do not jump they will break.

This makes Sir Spurde the leader of a devoted band of followers who know that by following him they are unlikely to have to do more than step delicately over the smashed and shattered remains of a fence.

Now all this is very jolly, but whatever people may think, the primary purpose of a fence is not as a subject for hunting people to tell the most dreadful porkies about; no, they are there to prevent farm stock getting from the field where they are supposed to be, into the field where there is some very good agricultural reason why they should not be. This means that hunts have to take damage very seriously to keep the good will of the farming community.

Many hunts now employ full-time fencing men who whizz round on hunting days in a truck full of rails, posts, hammers, saws, nails and what have you. Temporary repairs can be made on the spot, to keep the field stockproof until the next day when a more permanent job can be done. It is not unknown for timid tail-enders to come upon, not the nice gap they had been fervently hoping for, but a brand new, oven-fresh, set of rails where the gap was and that dratted fencing truck just squirting away down the lane.

I once hunted a country where our big riding day was a Friday. We had a fencing man out hunting, but I fully expected that he and I and various others would spend the thick end of each Saturday putting things to rights. There was one farm in the middle of the Friday country that I reckon we completely re-fenced during the years I was there. The nice man who farmed the land was not a hunting man but he said he was always pleased to see us. He reckoned that we left the place better than we found it and he never needed to do any fencing for the rest of the year.

The normal way of repairing a gap in a fence is to put a nice solid post and rails in the gap: it should look good and do good. Because of this preoccupation with gaps and repairs, I often used to have a few stakes and rails in the back of the pick-up.

I once went to a farm to pick up a dead calf. The farmers were mountainous twin brothers. They were enormous but gentle people to whom words were a carefully horded commodity. Whenever I went to the farm, they always seemed to be standing in the yard leaning on their prongs (pitch forks). They would watch beaming in a kindly fashion as I manhandled whatever carcase they might have had onto the truck. It was not that they did not want to help me, it was just that I would be long gone before the idea would have occurred to them.

On this day I had loaded the calf and the brothers ambled over to have a look at it and see if it looked any different, I suppose. There were some fencing stakes in the back of the truck.

One brother prodded a stake with an immense finger. "You be gwain to do some fencing then?"

I was maybe just a little put out at having to struggle unaided yet again, so I replied, "No, those are for my supper." This rather stupid remark was received with the totally blank silence which it deserved, so I climbed into the cab and was just about to start when I was startled by a strange deep roaring sound. The brothers were laughing: deep calling unto deep: bassoon in harmony with tuba.

"Zteak Zupper!" they bellowed, "'em gwain to 'ave a zteak zupper. *Haw! Haw! Haw! Haw!* " I left them clinging to each other in the middle of the yard, with tears running down their faces, pounding each other on the back and booming, "Zteak Zupper! Zteak Zupper!"

The cutting power of my tongue terrifies me sometimes.

All Backwoodsmen are tolerably weatherproof. They will, sometimes, get wet and cold in the pursuance of their lawful occasions. That does not mean that they enjoy getting wet and cold (well, I mean, who does), it is just that if you spend a great deal of time in the big outdoors, the Clerk of the Weather is going to feel liverish and dump on you every now and again. Therefore Backwoodsmen spend a great deal of time, trouble and not a little money trying to find the perfect combinations of clothing that will keep the weather out and the heat of the body in.

Over the years I have tried endless combinations of clothing. I have tried rubber, plastic, waxed cotton, polyunsaturates, the lot: none of them works. That is not entirely true. You can buy, for instance, an oilskin (PVC now I suppose) suit as worn by trawler men and it will keep you dry as a bone as long as you stand stock still. As soon as you move and generate a little heat, you will get perspiration and then condensation, which the ever-so-efficient PVC will ever so efficiently keep in. The end result is that you finish up as wet and clammy as you would have been had you bared your body to the elements.

One of the things that you do not want to do on the Northumbrian hills in January is much baring of the body to the elements. A Northumbrian hill wind in a sour mood is quite something else. It can lift the fillings out of your teeth and shrivel you like a piece of overcooked bacon. Every year there are cases of unwary people who set out onto the hills improperly clad, thinking that because they are nice and warm in a sheltered spot near sea level, they will be just as warm at 2,000 feet in the teeth of the wind. As a rule of thumb, the temperature drops one degree for every 300 feet of height and the wind can make the chill factor into a telephone number (local call, of course).

The thing to remember is that there is no way that you can keep totally *dry* and totally *warm*. The thing to concentrate on is keeping warm. So you need something that will baffle the wind and absorb the moisture. We are talking natural fibres: layers of wool/cotton are what are needed. A good hunt coat turns the weather well, but sadly the modern cloth is not what it was. I had some red coats made of the pre-Hitler war cloth. It was so hard and stiff that the coats would nearly stand up on their own and you needed a sail maker's palm to get a needle through the cloth. Those coats really did keep the weather out. They were irreplaceable and I mourned their final demise from old age.

The problem with a hunt coat is that there is a limit to the number of layers that you can get underneath them. Now that I have retired from the horse, I am no longer limited by the conventions of sartorial taste and rectitude. I travel the hills on Rupert my ATV in total comfort and warmth.

How is this achieved you may ask (you were going to ask, I feel sure). The answer is: Layers.

Now I never wear vests; you may please yourself. You may hear people talk about thermal underwear: very warm I grant you, but it smells. You may say that it is unlikely that anyone is going to get close enough to your underwear on a Northumbrian hilltop to be worried by malodour. That is certainly a point of view to consider, but I always live in hope.

Passing quickly on, we come to a good thick shirt (wool or cotton) tucked well down into a pair of good roomy plus-fours: always very comfortable garments and very practicable should you want to carry a ferret down the leg.

Below the plus-fours we come to immensely thick woollen stockings, which in turn peep coyly over the top of thermal boots from Sweden made of reindeer hide. Warm feet are the basis of righteousness.

Upwards we now go and come to several layers of woollen sweater, beneath a thick loden coat; then a scarf and the topping is supplied by the sort of hat that has ear flaps that you can tie under the chin.

So you see that I am not only warm but environmentally friendly, on the basis that, were I to hand in my dinner pail on the hill, everything that I was wearing would be degradable along with my cadaver and nothing would be left blowing about to offend the National Park Authority.

Ah, you say, but all that wool is not waterproof. True, but it will absorb an awful lot of moisture (both ways) and you will still be warm, even if you are wet.

I would have to say that when I am fully dressed for the rigours of the hill, I do look a bit like the Michelin Man, but the only bit of me that is still open to the elements, as it were, is the nose, which might turn a little blue on occasion. However, as I am able to carry a thermos with me on the machine, I can always steam it a bit.

In fact so warm and comfortable am I that I am able to take a very relaxed view of a day of appalling weather.

On a recent hunting day I was sitting on top of the Ewe Hill whilst a black north-westerly gale was howling around me and buffeting me impotently and impertinently. I just turned my back on it and was happily munching a sandwich and supping a cup of tea when one of the Lady Joint Masters hove in sight. She was a Blue Lady. I do not just mean that she was unhappy (although this undoubtedly seemed to be the case), but that all the parts that I could see were blue: how far up or down the blueness went is not for me to say.

She was cold and miserable, she said; everybody was cold and miserable; the hounds were cold and miserable and it was obvious that the foxes had decided not to come out and play anyway; could they not go home?

Go home? Well really, I had never heard such nonsense. Cold, wet and miserable? Of course they were cold, wet and miserable, that is what people go out hunting for, to be cold, wet and miserable. It would never have been an acceptable reason for going home when I was hunting hounds. I had never heard such pathetic, wimpish nonsense. Go home, indeed! Why, I remembered the time when (on just such a day as this in January) I fell in the river Dart, right under; horse and all. I just lay on the bank with my feet in the air to drain the water out of my boots; leaped on my horse and on with the hunt. Never thought of going home.

Then there was another time . . . I paused at this point to pour myself another cup of steaming tea and looked up. The Lady Joint Master had gone home, and taken the hounds with her. I really do not know what things are coming to.

The thought of hounds makes me think about worming. My thought association with any animal is immediately: "when have I got to dose it?" I think we have already discussed my perennial preoccupation with the wily nematode who, left to his own devices, will brutally bore through the bowels of sheep. The canine internal plumbing also needs continuous maintenance and the fact is that most people do not worm their hounds/dogs half often enough.

The worming of hounds these days is a doddle, what with all the new-fangled drugs and what have you. When I was a young man the situation was different and fraught with difficulty. In those days and indeed until fairly recent times, the glorious specific for hounds was Arica Nut Powder.

I have absolutely no idea what an Arica Nut looks like, or where it comes from. However, I can tell you that when ground up into a powder it closely resembles Cocoa, but it ain't the same thing at all.

The important thing with dosing is to see that each individual gets a proper share. What we used to do was to mix the Arica Nut Powder with Syrup of Buckthorn (Why? Oh dear, I do not know. If you asked one of the old school huntsman a question like that, he would growl: "Because I tell you to, boy, and look lively,") and lard. You mixed it up into a nice thick paste with your fingers and then rolled the paste out into balls, about the size of a gobstopper. They actually look rather appetising: rather like those chocolate truffle things. *But* you should not be led astray and allow yourself to do what a friend of mine did. In an absent-minded moment he licked his fingers. Oh dear, oh dear; you may have learnt at school that perpetual motion is mathematically impossible. The Friend very nearly disproved that theory. From which you may have gathered that Arica Nut Power is fast acting and very efficient and pretty rough stuff. Indeed, I knew one old hunt servant who was plagued with gut trouble all his life. He put this down to the fact that his father, who was also a huntsman, used to administer a worm-ball to his children whenever he wormed his hounds.

Administering a worm-ball to a child is not quite the same thing as administering a worm-ball to a hound. It is actually a very simple process: you just open the hound's mouth and poke the worm-ball down the back of its throat with a finger. Any finger will do — depending on how many you have left at your disposal. You see the trouble is that whilst you know that you are doing good to the hound, the hound may not realise it and does not necessarily want to be done good to anyway. Indeed, many human beings can be exceptionally difficult in this respect. Those who have worked with hounds know that in many respects they are more human than many humans, except that they have bigger and sharper teeth.

February

Backwoodsmen are caring people. They deplore the state of the world, which they very properly blame on politicians and bureaucrats. Politicians and bureaucrats occupy spaces in Backwoods demonology somewhere between rats and carrion crows. Backwoodsmen strongly disapprove of the activities of all vermin and are strongly in favour of law and order, but they are not easily shocked. However, there are certain crimes so ghastly and so heinous that even the most hardened and calloused Backwoodsman may well blench beneath his wind-reddened and weather-beaten exterior.

One of the crimes that comes in this category is Vulpicide. A true and proper Backwoodsman regards the fox almost as a sacred animal to be protected and looked after. The Backwoodsman will always be pleased should he meet a fox whilst going about his daily business and will normally raise his hat to it; metaphorically if necessary. The exception to this rule is on hunting days. Then the Backwoodsman will pursue the fox with the utmost vigour and do everything possible to see that his hounds catch the beggar, whilst applying the proper rules of sportsmanship, of course. The Backwoodsman finds absolutely nothing strange, or contradictory, in this attitude. The pursuit of the fox with a properly conducted pack of hounds is meet, right and the bounden duty of all Backwoodsmen.

The Termination with Extreme Prejudice of a fox in any other way is vulpicide and is very properly regarded as a black crime by all right-thinking countrymen.

It is a sad thing, and very melancholy, that there are now creatures living in the countryside who are so sunk in the lust of the slaughter of tame pheasants and the accretion of lucre that they not only tacitly condone vulpicide, but actually encourage it. It is my contention that when the shooting season finishes, at the end of January, all gamekeepers should be kept firmly chained up in their kennels until the following autumn. I am not suggesting that they should not be taken for proper walkies and, of course, they should be given a modicum of food and water, but they should be *contained*. This strict treatment has become necessary because regrettably, very few employers have any control over their gamekeepers at all; indeed, they are positively terrified of them. There are few more revolting sights than a man cringing submissively before his servants, but that is the position adopted by many shooting men today. In fairness, it has to be said that many shooters of today are newcomers both to sport and to the countryside. I am reminded of the old beater who was asked by a gun if he had seen the "other gentlemen" and who gave the devastating reply:

"Gentlemen? I ain't seen a Gentleman on this shoot these last twenty-five years." *Eheu fugaces*.

Not even Backwoodsmen are immune from this weakness. When confronted with their crime they look shifty and start getting pompous about "Maximising the return on their assets." What they really mean is that they have found that they can make silly money by rearing battery pheasants and flogging days' shooting to the Frogs and Krauts, not to mention Porky Purveyors of Prophylactics.

Right-thinking Backwoodsmen are still unanimous in their condemnation of vulpicide.

Some years ago, a February day of unusually brutal wind and sleet had driven me into the Squire and Strumpet for a warm.

Mrs Tucker was busily polishing glasses behind the bar, but being a quiet weekday morning there was no one else about, except for a Pint of Bitter reading a newspaper in the corner. When I say "no one", I do not mean to say that Fred and Ned were not draped over opposite ends of the bar, but they were as much part of the fixtures and fittings as the clock and the picture of Mrs Tucker's father in the uniform and waxed moustache with which he had relieved Mafeking (with a little help from General Roberts). No, what I am trying to get through to you, if you would only listen and stop peering at the pictures on the wall, is that the Pint of Bitter with the newspaper was a *stranger*.

Fred and Ned and I were soon rattling the small change of rural conversation, as it might be:

"So I said to 'ee . . ."

"'Er said to I . . ."

"That fair tatered the varmint, I can tell 'ee . . ."

"Thic old van were parked behind Rose Cottage all thic night. 'Ee reckoned 'ee were fixing 'er plumbing . . . left 'is pipe wrench be'ind . . . immersion 'eater! Haw! Haw! Haw!"

Mrs Tucker was tut-tutting and well-I-never-didding when the door blew open with a tremendous crash and in came a blast of wind, a shower of sleet and Jim Varco in an oilskin coat and a rage.

"They blighters!" he roared, "they blighters!" as he put his massive shoulder to the door and drove the wind and sleet back with it. "Oi'll get they Buggers!"

"What hever's the matter, Jim?" said Mrs Tucker hastily putting a double rum and pep on the bar. Jim shook himself like a huge shaggy dog and sprayed us all with droplets. He downed the drink in one massive swallow and put the glass back on the bar for replenishment.

"Do 'ee knaw what they buggers have done? They'm only shot a fox and hung the wretch on my gate; now then?" We greeted this pronouncement with the stunned silence that it deserved. In those far off days, there was little crime in our community and this made the shock and horror more acute. To think that amongst us there lurked one so base of instinct as to stoop to vulpicide. To pile the Pelion of indignity upon the Ossa of skulduggery, they had hung the corpse upon the gate of Jim Varco, Honorary Terrier Man to our hunt and a Man of Respect. This was indeed crime of the grossest sort.

Ned was the first to recover.

"Well, 'tis like this yere. There's never no good comes to they as puts off foxes. Why I remember a man over to Six Lanes, well, 'ee shot a fox an' 'tweren't a week till 'is best cow died; there now". We all digested this example of crime and quite obviously related retribution with some satisfaction.

Then Fred took a hand. "I'll tell better than that. I mind the time one of they Scantlebury boys sniggled a fox and the next day, the very next day, mind, 'is wife run off with the worm drench rep; 'tis true."

This was a truly satisfying example of the marital knot being severed by the sword of Damocles and we all savoured it in silence until the rustling of a newspaper reminded us that there was a stranger in our midst.

"Excuse me," said the Pint of Bitter, "but I could not help overhearing your conversation." This was not unreasonable as the conversation had been conducted at the pitch and force required of such a drama. "Tell me, did the wife ever return?"

"'Er never did that I yeard tell."

The man folded his newspaper neatly and drained his pint. "Ah," he said, "well, in that case, I wonder if you gentlemen would be so good as to direct me to somewhere where I can shoot a fox."

February is a fairly quiet time in the Backwoods. I have even heard rumours of certain friends who go ski-ing in February. As is the custom when one hears disquieting rumours about the behaviour of friends, one sucks one's teeth and does one's best to understand and protect them from public opprobrium. In private one may do one's best to make them see the error of their ways and to persuade them gently into the paths of righteousness once more.

Ski-ing is not a Backwoodsmanly occupation, unless of course you happen to live in the sort of Backwoods where it is a necessary form of transport. The sort of ski-ing that involves going to those frightful clip joints in Switzerland, France and other such places is really only suitable for Rich White Trash and Secretaries from Sidcup and jolly good luck to them say I.

I go boarhunting in France in February. This is an Approved Backwoods Activity, but is outside the scope of this book which is meant to confine itself to matters British.

Nothing much is happening on the farm in February. The ewes are snugly tucked up in the shed and require only routine care and maintenance.

Hunting continues. In fact, February is one of my favourite hunting months. At this time the dog foxes travel great distances to work their wicked way with the vixens and if your hounds happen to drop in on an amorous visitor he will immediately pull up his trousers and head for home without bothering to adjust his dress. This makes for long, fast, straight hunts which may well take you into the territory of a neighbouring hunt, a process which I regard as being very good for discipline and the fostering of good sporting relationships with the neighbours.

Some years ago I had just such a hunt. It was one of those lovely hunts when hounds keep going and going at just the right speed. The speed that allows you to gallop on with them and enjoy every twist and turn of their work without them going so fast that you cannot keep in touch with them. This was just as well as the hunt involved some very steep gallops down and, by virtue of the fact, some gruelling pulls up the other side. All the time, the sight and the sound of hounds urged us on.

There is a certain stage in a hunt when it passes from being just another hunt into being a HUNT. This is the moment when you realise that this hunt is going to be underlined in red in the hunting diary. On this particular day, it came about when we crossed the steep valley into the neighbouring country and, with each successive hill, probed deeper and deeper into it. So deep into it, in fact, that I realised that we were nearing the place where the neighbours were hunting that day and I had to ponder the possibility of running into them. I also pondered the welcome I would undoubtedly receive from my some-what volcanic opposite number.

It was therefore with some relief, as we topped the next hill, that we saw the neighbour's hound van driving up the valley road towards their kennels. They had packed up and gone home. The coast was clear.

My dears, how we frolicked along the hill. We had only to breast the next hill and my neighbour's house would be in sight, which I thought would be rather jolly but, as it happened, the hounds ran into their fox in the valley.

We were miles from home and it seemed sensible to

take hounds and horses down to a farm in the valley and put them up there whilst transport was arranged. My horse had lost a shoe and so we lagged behind a bit down the valley road. I could see a little group formed at the farm, centred on the unmistakable figure of my neighbour. As I approached, the group seemed to evaporate. For some reason all the onlookers had taken themselves behind a large stone wall; the only sign of their continued presence was a row of caps peeking over the coping stones.

The Neighbour and I were left in a one-to-one situation. I thought how nice it was of him to come out and share in our jollification.

Let me say at once that I have every sympathy with him. A bad day's hunting is always a dispiriting thing. The very best thing that you can do is settle into a friend's armchair, and his whisky, and thus soothe one's unquiet spirit. The thing you do not need is for your friend's wife to come in and tell you that the next door hunt is squandering all over the hill behind your house. In such a circumstance you are perfectly entitled to rise six feet vertically from a sitting start and form a mushroom cloud. In such circumstances, I also would feel a little irritated and justified in stamping about seeing whom I might devour.

It is a good thing to get these little irritations off one's chest and a fat, smug, smirking slob who has just galloped all over your country and killed a fox practically on your back door step is an absolutely ideal target.

Such things make a day memorable and are a thread of gold running through the rich tapestry of rural life.

★   ★   ★

What taxes the intellectual capacity of the Backwoodsman through the long February nights? you may ask. Well, what about "the Servant Problem". I have to say that this problem does not worry Backwoodsmen as once it might have done. I felt very sorry for the venerable member of the genus whom I overheard complaining that he was "down to his last butler", but we have not had a butler in the family since the Hitler War. I do not really see much scope for one in my set-up at the moment. For one thing, my wine cellar is far too small to cope with two determined men.

I am reminded of the elderly Bachelor Backwoodsman who had an extensive and highly-valued cellar, together with an extensive and highly-valued old butler. They were almost as extensive and highly valued as his hatred for his heir. The heir consoled himself with the thought of the wondrous sluicing he would be able to indulge himself in when Uncle Bertie finally fell off his perch.

Alas, alas, the vain desires of man. The heir came rubbing his hands and maybe salivating a little into the cellar (mysteriously unlocked) the day after the funeral and found a comatose and very extensive butler and some 10,000 empty bottles. The old master had decreed that not a drop was to pass the generation gap and Master and Man had managed to get through the lot in twelve years. Such devotion to duty is rarely found these days.

I must confess that I would love to have a man to drive me about and clean my shoes and tell people on the telephone that they are very sorry but the master is at his dinner, so bog off (not that he would actually say the last bit you understand; it would be the way he said it).

I did have a chauffeur for a time; of a sort. He was a

marvellous chap who came to me as terrier man/ kennelman. He was also a mechanical genius — and I use the word advisedly.

I came upon him one day kicking my rather rusty Mini van in a gloomy sort of way. "Not much of a car for a Master," he said.

The truthful response to that would have been that I was not much of a master, and was skint to boot. I put this point to him as delicately as I could. He grunted.

The Genius used to spend most of his spare time ferreting about in the local scrapyard. He came back one day and said that he had found me a "proper car". It was a 1947 Wolseley, like the police cars in the old Ealing comedies: leather upholstery, walnut dashboard, ran like a Rolex, and could still do a ton without effort. It cost me the princely sum of £35.

This lovely car had one bad defect: it attracted the Old Bill like ferrets to a rabbit hole. I was forever being stopped at night. Large men in blue would prowl round the car "lovely bit of craftmanshipping"; "you don't see many like this nowing" and "I remember when I was on the Metting". They would then apologise for stopping me and wish me a safe journey home. All very nice, but the breathalyser had just come in and it was all rather unnerving.

The Genius solved the problem. Now that I had a proper car, he was quite happy to be seen in public with me. For ten shillings a night, he undertook to convey me anywhere, but things had to be done properly in a proper car. He insisted that I sat in the back whilst he drove wearing a Southend Corporation Bus driver's hat.

There are many substantial farmhouses in this part of

the world: "far ower big" for modern needs, but of course in the old days the big hill farms would have carried big staffs and the unmarried lads and lasses would have "lived in" (carefully separated, I need hardly add).

Great store was set by the quality of the food for those who lived in. To work in a "grand meat hoose" was a consummation devoutly to be wished. I remember an old friend of mine in Devon who had a small racing stable as well as a farm. I used to go to luncheon there occasionally and, as well as the family, six or ten lads would sit down. I have never before, or since, seen such huge joints of meat as used to appear on the sideboard. You would be unfortunate indeed to rise hungry from that table.

Not everyone was so lucky and not every employer so generous: High Starveasy was a case in point.

Postie was climbing the track to Starveasy early one morning when he met the shepherd lad legging it down the road with his box on his back.

"Ye're flitting?" said Postie who liked to keep his finger on the local pulse and have some titbits with which to regale his cronies in the Jolly Huntsman.

"Aye," said the lad stopping for a blow.

"Ye're no waiting on your breakfast then?" Starveasy and its owner were notorious for poor fare but even so it is a serious thing for a man to miss his breakfast. The lad explained that there was little meat to be had at Starveasy unless a ewe dropped dead on the turnip breaks when there would be a brief spate of mutton chops. When the pig drowned, there was a sudden rush of sausages for a spell.

Yes, yes and now?

"Weel, the auld wifie deed the nicht and arm no waiting to see what's for breakfast the morn."

You might think that with all these yong men and women under one roof romance would blossom and of course it did, human nature being what it is. With the strict supervision that was in force there was little room for hanky panky in any generation except this one, it having been entirely invented in the 1960s; at least you would think so to hear people go on about it.

Once upon a time there was a young horseman; which being interpreted meant that he was a man employed to work with the farm horses, which I am sure comes as a great surprise to you. Our young friend was employed on a big farm and, being a single lad, he lived in.

Also living and working in the house (in the dairy) was a maid. She was a fair but fickle creature and for a time she allowed her languorous gaze to fall favourably upon the young horseman, who became thoroughly smitten in his somewhat clumsy, tongue tied way.

The course of love seldom runs smoothly. The blockage in this particular amorous fuel line was occasioned by the arrival of a new shepherd lad. This newcomer was a creature of unusual sophistication. He greased his hair, knew how to dance the Black Bottom, and, *mirabile visu*, owned a primitive motor bicycle. Mounted on this machine with his cap turned back to front and a rakish pair of goggles, the young shepherd was the very epitome of raw sexual power (although we must bear in mind that such a thing was not going to be invented for another forty years, or so) and represented a gross temptation to the wandering attentions of the fair but fickle Dairymaid.

Not to put too fine a point on it, she dumped the Horse Lad like a cart load of manure. She left him to grind his teeth on his old push bike, whilst she whizzed off, on the pillion of the shepherd's motor bicycle, to whatever fleshpots the local area offered.

At this stage in the story it is necessary to reintroduce the Carbide Lamp. The Carbide Lamp was a primitive form of bicycle lamp, not terribly effective but good enough to wobble home from the Two Happy Haemorrhoids by. To the best of my knowledge and belief the lamps worked thus:

A lump of carbide was placed in the bottom of the lamp. Water was allowed to drip onto the carbide. This produced a gas which could be ignited to produce a feeble light. It also produced a monstrous SMELL.

The Horseman felt that he had been hard done by, having had his sincere and simple passion dumped back in his lap and having to face the daily presence of his Old Flame and her new lump of Carbide (if you see what I mean).

The Horseman held his council, but determined on Revenge.

The single girls slept in a sort of dormitory, firmly separated by the quarters of the farmer and his wife from the sleeping place of the single men at the other end of the house.

In those simple days there was not much in the way of household amenities and plumbing.

For major catharses you trolled down to the little shed at the bottom of the garden and made use of a basic system which was referred to as "a bucket and a burying".

For night time emergencies, the need was met by the good, old fashioned chamber pot under the bed.

At a time of day when the house was still and empty, the Horseman came by stealth to the maids' room and placed a lump of carbide in the pot under the bed of the Fair and Fickle One.

There is no need for us to go into great scatological detail. Suffice it to say that at some period during the night a chemical reaction took place in the maids' room and there was a release of noxious gas in the confined space.

The choking cloud brought the occupants coughing, spluttering and wailing onto the landing.

The cloud came with them and went frolicking on into the main house allowing the farmer and his family to participate in the fun.

Through all the tumult and the shouting the Horseman slept happily in his little bed far away at the other end of the house. His sleep was the sleep of the just: he who has just pulled a major stroke.

There is little doubt that the motor car is at one and the same time a blessing and a curse for rural social life. It is a blessing because it makes it easier to go out for a jolly. It is a curse because if there were no motor cars then you could not be breathalysed. I believe that you can be charged as being drunk in charge of a horse, under an act of 1895: I understand that the maximum fine is thirty shillings and I have never actually heard of anyone being prosecuted under it.

As a very young Master of Hounds I hunted a wild hill country. Far out in the hills there farmed a family, two brothers and a sister. I do not think that one brother and the sister ever left the farm. Once a month Dunc, the second brother, would mount his shaggy pony, sling a bag over his back for the shopping and set out to town.

He would visit the mart, have his hair cut, do the shopping and then retire to the Station Hotel for "a bit of dinner". "Dinner" went on from 12 noon to the far end of 12 midnight, or whatever mine Host would stand for, or until such time as Duncan sank quietly beneath the table. This he used to do with the minimum fuss and with a beatific smile on his face. Nobody minded because he was such a nice man, drunk or sober, and never a bit of trouble.

At chucking-out time, the regulars would pick up Dunc and his bag and carry him out to the stable where the old pony had been munching quietly through the day. Dunc would be plonked on the pony and his feet securely fastened under the pony's belly with baler twine. The pony would be led outside, given a slap on the rump and it would go titt-upping away into the night.

Up the long lane the little pony would trot with his slumbering cargo, out across the moor track, through the stack yard gate and into his home stable where a good feed awaited him in the manger.

The sister who had been sitting by the kitchen range would light the lamp and come across the yard. She would cut the twine and Dunc would slide gently down into the thick straw of the stable where he would lie snoring contentedly until morning.

That is the great thing about a horse, you see, it will

always take you home. Not even the most sophisticated modern car has gaffered that problem yet.

A horse and cart is an even better form of conveyance should you be a little "market peart". The lads can lay you out in the back and put the pig net over you and set the old horse heading for home.

Even this low tech, and environmentally sensitive, form of transport, however, could have its problems.

Let us consider the plight of my old friend Farmer Rundle. Old Jim Rundle would go every week to the town in his smart trap with Denis his smart old cob. In those days, it was an attractive little town; it is now an Urban Resettlement Area, the Station Hotel is now the Pop Inn and the stables have been converted into an health food bar and solarium.

Anyway, back to happier times. The Station Hotel had spacious parking and stabling facilities: Denis would be put into the stable and the trap would be parked in the yard with all the others. Farmer Rundle would attend to his business at the mart and then return to the hotel for "a bit of dinner". We have already discussed this "bit of dinner" business so you will not be surprised to hear that it was black night when Farmer Rundle made his somewhat unsteady way across the yard to retrieve Denis and attach him once more to the trap for the homeward journey.

Oh Dear! Oh Lord! What is this? Denis is already harnessed to the trap! Which is all very fine except that Denis and the trap are both *inside* the stable.

It may be that some of you have tried to get a trap through a stable door and if you have not, then you will just have to take my word for it that trap into stable will not go; certainly not in the normal way. To enstable a trap you have to take the wheels off, turn it on its side, carry it through the door, then you can turn it right way up, put the wheels back on, and harness the horse to it. You are then confronted with the problem of getting the complete equipage out again.

Who would do such a thing? Well, the burden of suspicion must fall squarely on the brawny shoulders of "they bliddy Pascoe Boys — the bliddy young hellers" who can even now be heard bellowing with mirth from somewhere in the surrounding darkness.

In case you think that this particular form of rural humour went out with the horse and cart, I have to tell you that it survived through several Socialist governments and the worst excesses of the Welfare State.

I was once the proud owner of a Messerschmitt. Do not think Battle of Britain — think Bubble Cars. The Messerschmitt was the kind of long narrow bubble car which carried two people one behind the other, instead of the more usual side by side. You got into it by lifting the perspex cockpit lid and shoe-horning yourself into the seat. It was rather fun to drive — when it went. It had a distressing propensity to stop and sulk, preferably on some remote stretch of road in the middle of the night and most especially when it was raining. As an example of German technical expertise it was a frost.

The Messerschmitt had two other major disadvantages.

At that time there were still a lot of relics from the Battle of Britain. They used to have huge ginger moustaches and those old Bentleys with straps over the bonnet. The sight of a Messerschmitt (any Messerschmitt) was too much for them. There I would be trolling peacefully along to, as it might be, Guildford, when suddenly eeeeeooooooGH! pocketa — pocketa — pocketa! The whole strap-bonneted, ginger-moustached might of Umpteen Squadron would descend upon me — horns blaring, eyes staring, head lights flashing. It got very, very wearing.

The other major disadvantage of the Messerschmitt was its lightness.

I went to an inter-hunt darts match one night. A good time was had by all, but when I came out my Messerschmitt had flown. I do not know whether any of you have been faced with the problem of getting a bubble car off the flat roof of a public house lavatory. I am here to tell you that it is not easy. I had been well and truly Rundled.

"I knaw 'tis you bliddy Pascoe Boys. I can yere 'ee laffing out there. You bliddy hellers . . ."

Two things that greatly exercise Backwoodsmen in the dark days of winter are fires and baths.

Every Backwoodsmanly kitchen is likely to have a Rayburn or an Aga; Backwoods Ladies do not really believe that it is possible to cook properly on anything else. The sensible Backwoodsman does not argue about this and certainly does not get himself embrangled in the details of the kitchen. He knows that the real purpose of the Aga/Rayburn is to have a rail in front of the stove on which he can warm his bum whilst having the first cup of tea on a cold dark winter's morning.

The other advantage of these stoves is that they have a good bottom oven which is handy for warming up hypothermic lambs, but this does not really concern us at the present time.

Backwoodsmen all got very excited when continental wood-burning stoves appeared over here. I was no exception and had a monstrous thing installed. There is no doubt that wood-fired heating is a tremendously good idea, always provided that (a) you live in the middle of a forest, (b) you have a man with a chain saw doing nothing else but cut up the log supply for the year after next and (z) that you have next year's supply maturing nicely in a huge airy wood shed. In the case where you are unable to meet any of these criteria then you should spit out the wood-burning stoves, pay the Arabs and burn oil.

When you buy your wood-burning stove you will get a driver's handbook which has been translated from the French via Swedish, or, as it might be, from the Swedish via the French. Whatever, it is more than possible that you will have wearied of Euro-gobble long before you get to the small print — always supposing that you bother to read the handbook at all. (As my old father always used to say: "As a last resort read the instructions.") Somewhere buried deep in the fine print you will find a cautionary statement that only wood that has been cut and seasoned for at least a year is recommended for use in your wood-burning apparatus. The penalty for using green wood is tar.

We got tar on Christmas Eve. We came in from hunting to a cold kitchen over the floor of which an evil tide of black goo was spreading. The chimney was blocked solid. It was not a happy Christmassy prospect, but thanks to the Great and Good Mr Johnson (Plumber Extraordinary) order was restored.

We moved house shortly afterwards. It seemed the best way to get rid of the stove.

One of the things that a Backwoodsman looks forward to when he comes in with the February chill eating into his bone marrow is a good hot bath.

The Hunting Backwoodsman (deep frozen) who finds that his wife's shooting friends have used all the hot water is liable to express his displeasure in a pithy and uninhibited manner. He will feel especially peeved as he knows that shooters drive everywhere in tropically-heated and hermetically-sealed Range Rovers. He also knows that, at a hint of rain or the threat of a speck of mud, they will flee, shrieking hysterically, to a centrally-heated bothy. There they will guzzle and glug for the rest of the day, firmly resisting all efforts to get them out into the nasty fresh air again. Such people do not deserve hot baths. They are quite soft enough as it is.

The Hot Bath is an important part of the hunting day. It is much more important than just being an agency for washing. This side is important, however; warm up an unwashed foxhunter and you will have an interesting olfactory experience.

It is a moment of exquisite agony when you first dip a toe that you have long since ceased to feel into the steaming depths. Inch (*Oo!*) by inch (*Aah!*) the body is inserted, until at last there is that supreme moment when the hot water closes over the whole massive bulk (*Coooorgh!*).

The floating pillow should then be inserted behind the head.

The wireless should be turned to something congenial.

A very brown whisky and soda should come easily to hand.

The sponge should be floating conveniently.

Dogs that wind up and swim about the bath and/or submarines that sink when you press a bulb are optional but will mark out a true Backwoodsman from the Common Herd.

Once the chap is wallowing nicely and everything is to hand, he should immediately start reviewing the events of the day whilst the details are still fresh in his mind. An old foxhunter once said that no huntsman should go to sleep on the night after a day's hunting without analysing his day's performance in minute detail and deciding exactly the moment when each fox was lost — or even won. The bath is an ideal environment for this intellectual exercise, which should be pursued with the utmost rigour.

The day's performance having been evaluated, the bather may then be permitted a little relaxation. He may listen to the Archers and ponder on the suburbanisation of this once excellent programme and wonder what on earth the Agricultural Story Editor does to earn his, no doubt, exorbitant fee. It is quite obvious that the A.S.E. knows nothing about sheep. Sheep should be excluded from the Archers because the local standards of Flockmanship are obviously abysmal. For instance, how can it be that a man putatively so go ahead as Brian Aldridge has no proper sheep-handling system? He has no weighing crate, no handling race and no shedder. To draw his lambs for the mart, they have to be chased round the pen and manhandled. This causes uneconomic stress on the lambs and apparently requires the participation of half the cast. To judge from the way they pant and groan, they are also undergoing an unacceptable amount of stress. Oh dear, oh dear; still, it gives the wallowing Backwoodsman a chance to indulge in hoots of derision which always sound better in the peculiar accoustics that bathrooms have. In fact I think that the Archers require a Backwoods Story Editor. None of the present characters are recognisable countrymen: they are all what the Urban Mind thinks countrymen ought to be like.

Many Backwoodsmen will sing in the bath. I am a great Bathtime Baritone and I am quite certain that my warblings give immense pleasure to the household, in spite of their protestations to the contrary.

All duties having been discharged, then is the time to allow oneself to sink into a deep, steam-laden slumber, always hoping that the floating pillow will prevent one from terminal immersion.

This all takes some little time. An hour is the minimum time that should be allotted for a really meaningful bath. Anything less should be regarded as a purely functional lavatorial process and cannot be regarded as bathing within the meaning of the act.

We have forgotten to mention smelly things in the bath (apart from sweaty foxhunters that is). Backwoodsmen are very keen on pouring things in the bath. Things that make a nice smell, or give a bit of zip to the fatigued system. Best of all are those unguents which claim to relieve you of the chore of actually having to soap yourself all over and which cleanse you as you soak.

You would be well advised, however, to treat some Backwoodsly concoctions with care.

Time for a cautionary tale.

Once upon a time an American came to England on a hunting tour. As part of the tour he came to stay with a certain Backwoodsman who sent him out for a day with the Blankshire hounds from which he returned cold, wet and miserable. Those who know the Blankshire Hunt will tell you that cold, wet and miserable is the normal state of affairs with the Blankshire. (There is the story of the man who arrived to stay with the Master of the Blankshire who asked the visitor if he would like a drink. The visitor replied that he would like something "long, cold and full of gin", to which the master replied that his wife would be down in a minute but would the visitor like a drink whilst he was waiting.) But all that is by the by. Let us return to our Deep Frozen American.

The Backwoodsman sent him off to have a bath with instructions not to be too long as there were people coming in for drinks. As an afterthought, he handed the guest an anonymous black bottle with the instruction to "try a few drops of this in the bath".

The American commenced a luxurious soak and then realised that he had forgotten the black bottle and its contents.

I do not know how much contact you have had with the Cousins, but they all work on the principle that if one pill does you good then six pills must be better. Applying this principle, the American decanted a generous portion of the contents of the bottle into the bath . . .

Downstairs the drinking guests had started to arrive.

One of the guests was a man of ancient lineage and great personal charm and amiability. He also had what may best be described as "certain proclivities".

"*YAAAARRRRRGGGGHHHH!!!*"

All eyes in the hall turned upwards to the landing. There in capering agony was the totally naked, lobster-pink, protein-plump figure of a liniment-corroded American.

This vision was too much for the proclivities of the Man of Ancient Lineage. He put down his drink and leaped for the staircase. "I say," he said, "I say: Tally Ho! Jolly well Tally Ho!"

To achieve the happy state of proper bathing it is necessary to have a proper bath.

A proper bath is a hard-won article these days. You must forget all those nasty little plastic pots proferred by purveyors of sanitary ware. You must think Victorian and cast iron. The Victorians were the first people since Roman times to take bathing seriously: they thought in generous terms. They thought as I do that a bath is not just for washing, but is for stretching out and luxuriating in. In the craze for pastel-shaded plastic pulchritude these solid old baths went to the scrapyard in droves. Now they are inevitably coming back into fashion.

My quest for a proper bath took several years and, like most great discoveries, eventually came about by chance.

One fine spring morning in Yorkshire I paused in my peregrination down a country lane to lean on a gate and look at someone else's sheep. Farmers spend a great deal of time leaning on other people's gates, looking at other people's stock. The fact that they would be better employed leaning on their own gate and looking at their own stock is neither here nor there. It is much more fun trying to detect the slightest flaw in someone else's business than it is redressing the glaring deficiencies in your own.

As a matter of record I could find little to fault in this flap of ewes and lambs, which was really rather irritating. I watched one fine-looking ewe as she wandered off towards the corner of the field. She was going for a drink.

My eye fell upon the drinking trough.

SHAZAM!

There it was.

A bath.

No: the bath.

No, no: *the bath.*

It was perfect: a huge, cast-iron Victorian Megabath; claw feet, the lot. It was just what I wanted.

Your average Yorkshire farmer is not a man given to displaying strong emotion or to making rash and hasty decisions. Mr Uldale removed his cap (this *was* in fact a display of strong emotion) and scratched his head.

"Thoo wants to buy t'ard bath?"

"Aye." It always pays to use the language of the country.

"T'ard bath in t'top field?"

"Aye."

"What dost thoo want it for?"

"A bath."

"A bath? For washing thissen in?"

"Aye."

"Th'art bluidy daft."

"Aye; happen yer reet."

"Ow much then?"

"Ten quid."

"Nay, nay, young man, that's a valuable bath is that: twenty-five."

"Twelve."

"Twenty."

"Fifteen."

He spat on his hand and offered it to me: "We're both

daft, tha knaws," he said.

Within a week the bath was cleaned up and plumbed in and being wallowed in. I have moved house three times since then and the bath has always come with me and is with me yet.

March

Things begin to wake up on the farm in March. The ewes are in an advanced state of pregnancy and are on a steadily increasing ration of concentrates, or "hand meat" if you prefer the vernacular. The slightest rustle of a bag in the shed produces an insistent chorus of greed.

Outside the shed there are also things to be done. I am not as busy as my arable brethren. As soon as the weather permits, they are whizzing about their spring cultivations and chucking fertiliser on anything and everything.

I am not a great fertiliser fiend. Every now and then I have my soil tested and if it needs lime to sweeten it, then I bung some on. If the Ph is getting a bit low then the land gets a slagging, which is not at all the same thing as you get from your mother-in-law.

By and large I rely on the magic of muck.

Every summer a man comes with a cunning machine with huge mechanical jaws and digs out the winter's compacted layers of sheep shit and straw. Fred and I lean on the gate, puff our pipes and watch. We calculate how long the job would take us with gripes (four-pronged forks) and a muck cart: the answer is considerably longer than it takes the man with his snarling bob cat grab. The muck is dumped outside the shed and rots peacefully during the summer and autumn, gaining in value and virtue all the time.

One frozen winter's day the man returns with grab and muck spreaders and all that lovely rotted-down goodness is scattered all over the fields.

Fred and I lean on the gate, puff our pipes and wonder how long that job would take us with horse and cart and gripe. The answer is much the same as it was the first time.

Come the spring, I actually do bestir myself and, as it happens, the remains of the muck.

March is dragging time.

Dragging, or chain harrowing, is an important part of grassland management. It breaks down the remains of the muck, pulls out all the old dead grass, and generally lets the light and air into the pastures: it is raking the lawn on a grand scale.

The first thing to do is to find the drag (or, as it might be, the chain harrows). These will almost certainly have been left in whatever remote portion of the farm you finished using them the previous March. They will have become overgrown with rubbish and weeds and will have disappeared into the landscape. I know that they should have been rolled up tidily and put away in a shed, but this is the real world we are talking about.

In the real world you probably rediscover your drags by tripping over them and badly bruising your shins. You then attach them to the drawbar of your tractor by a length of chain and begin, well, dragging.

Up and down the field you go, up and down; up and down; and, if you have time, you do it cross the way as well. You make pretty contrasting stripes as you go up and down with the drags clanking musically behind.

It is all very satisfying.

I certainly would not want to spend my every waking hour on a tractor as some people seem content to do, but I do enjoy a bit of tractor work now and then; especially on a nice day. No special, minute, accuracy is required for dragging. It is a simple and relaxing job.

Every now and then you can arise in the cab and adjust your dress. There is something about tractor seats that drives the underpants deep into the crutch, causing acute discomfort.

Once you are sitting comfortably, you may cast about for some agreeable way of passing the time. You may listen to the wireless. Please do not tell me that your tractor does not have a wireless. You will tell me next that you still work your ground with oxen. Of course the tractor has a wireless. You would not get many tractor drivers into the cab unless there is a wireless — but there is a problem. Most tractor wirelesses are permanently stuck on Radio One. With infinite patience and kindness you may just be able to coax them into accepting Radio Two, but Radios Three and Four are beyond the pale. No self-respecting tractor wireless would be seen dead with Three and Four. Should you be so crass and unfeeling as to try to force them into the realms of music and comprehensible speech, they become confused and ill and are likely to expire in a welter of terminal static. Those stations are just too difficult for the poor things.

In my case this problem has ceased to be a problem anyway. For some peculiar reason, my wireless was set on the shelf over one of the rear wheels where the collies tend to lie in transit. On a day of pouring rain, a collie who was for obvious reasons soaking wet, jumped into the cab and lay on top of the wireless. The poor thing drowned. I think that it had been thoroughly cowed by my attempts to listen to the Morning Story anyway. It was probably a merciful release.

You can do a lot of good thinking whilst you are chugging up and down on a tractor. You can think really deep thoughts, like for instance: the Meaning of Life, or what might be for supper. In fact, you can solve this last problem easily by getting Control on the Citizens' Band Radio. You did not know that there was such a thing in the tractor cab? Silly you: the modern Tractorist would rather his tractor lacked an engine than a Citizens' Band Radio. With this useful machine you can give the wife a "shout" (technical term) as follows:

"Snow White, Snow White," (that is her "handle" — technical term) "you got your ears on? Come back." This is a polite enquiry as to whether she is receiving you.

To which she should reply (always supposing that she has remembered to switch the blasted set on): "That's a Rog, Big Daddy (hello darling), you're ten-two (she can hear me well). What's your twenty (where are you)?" Well of course the silly moo knows that I am dragging in the Bank Field, but it is all part of the CB mystique. Anyway we "ratchet" (technical term for a bit of a chat) and I establish that it is sausage and mash (technical term for sausages and mashed potatoes) for supper to which I will give a big ten-four (jolly good), enjoin her to remain ten-ten (standing by) and wish her "Bysyby" which is one of the classic ways of ending your transmission. A whole new language, as you see, and not one that they taught at Eton in my day.

Citizens' Band is an open circuit so that you can listen to anyone talking on the same channel.

For many years I used Channel 14 but it became monopolised by a young couple who used it for their courting and would witter on for hours when I wanted to find out about the supper or have my bath run or whatever. So I changed to Channel 11. Do you know what? The same young bugger was on that one too, conducting an equally sickly courtship with another woman; quite disgraceful, as I hope you will agree.

The hot thing on 11 at the moment is the milkman who is always being sent despairing messages by his wife. She implores him to return for his dinner, tea, supper or whatever. He never replies. I cannot but think that I am "earwigging" (technical term) a sad little domestic drama here: why is the milkman so busy with his gold top that he never gets home for his meals? I cannot wait to find out.

"Big Daddy! Big Daddy! on channel?" I recognise the dulcet tones of "Polecat" alias my neighbour Jim, who I can see tractoring on the other side of the valley.

Jim is the very man to ask about the Meaning of Life; especially if Newcastle United lost (yet again) on the previous Saturday.

Should there be nothing else to engage my attention, then I can always sing, or recite poetry, and all the time the tractor chugs, the drags rattle and the cab reeks of tobacco and contentment. The nice thing about it is that this is *work* and I am enjoying it.

I suppose that it is an arguable point as to whether March is the last month of winter or the first month of spring. It is certainly a very fickle month, one which can lay a blizzard on you when, ten minutes before, you were panting in your shirt sleeves.

I have no doubt as to when spring starts. Spring starts when I hear the first curlew. These excellent birds spend their winters on the sea shores and estuaries, poking about with their long curved bills. In the spring they return to their breeding grounds, and their haunting whistle on the hills and moors tells you that spring is on the way, even if you are freezing your butt off at that particular moment.

Curlews will only nest in wild and relatively undisturbed places and there are many places in England now where they can no longer be heard. Their wild calling is one of my earliest memories and evokes memories of my Cornish childhood and a way of life that has gone for ever. So the curlew is special to me and I apply the curlew test to wherever I might consider living: if the curlews do not want to nest there, then neither do I.

Another thing that happens in March is that the Shepherds' Supper Season comes to an end. The proper title of these amazing happenings is "Shepherds' and Farmworkers' Suppers". They seem to be peculiar to the Northumbrian Cheviots and they are unlike anything that I have encountered anywhere else.

There are only four of them, each serving a separate region. I am privileged to attend two of them and I use the word "privileged" advisedly, because the places at these suppers are zealously sought after and many men have waited years for an opening.

Each supper is organised by its own committee. With what purpose? I hear you cry. Fun, my dear, fun; you should try it some time.

The last of these suppers happens in March. It takes place at a famous public house (we shall call it the Dandelion and Burdock, with which we became acquainted on New Year's Day) deep in the hills. It is the last great get together for the hill men before they get buried in the lambing. They put their hair in a figurative braid and come with the determination of enjoying themselves: this they usually seem to manage to achieve.

The suppers follow a traditional pattern.

Imagine, if you will, the large back room of a public house, or maybe a village hall. Here will be long rows of trestle tables such as might enable the emplacement of some 150 well-built men.

Men? Yes, of course men. You surely do not imagine that women get allowed to attend these happenings? This is Northumberland, mate, none of your Hampstead-pinko-freako attitudes up here; women forsooth!

But hang about! Of course there are women involved;

who do you think produces the substantial supper which is sat down to at 7.30 sharp? Who do you think serves it? Why, the wives and girlfriends of those happily chomping away, of course. Then when the women have done the washing up, they get hoyed out the door and sent home before the funny parts begin. We adhere to traditional standards up here in the north.

The evening follows a well-established pattern. The first thing to do after supper is to drink the health of Her Gracious Majesty so that we can all get the pipes and fags out; if smoking offends you, then this is not the place for you.

There will normally be four main speeches: toasts to Agriculture, Foxhunting, The Shepherds and Farm-workers, The Entertainers. Each toast has to have a reply so you do not have to be a mathematical genius to work out that we are looking at eight speeches. Between each speech there will be some form of entertainment: music, singing, story telling, poetry.

Now what in fact we are talking about is keeping 150 pretty independent-minded bottoms sitting uncomplainingly on pretty hard chairs for some four hours (with occasional refuelling and spring-easing pauses). To achieve this you require speakers and entertainers of the very highest order and a Chairman who commands great respect to keep the whole thing moving. Northumberland is able to supply all the necessary.

In the years that I have been attending Shepherds' Suppers I have endured very few bad speeches, and how many of you who attend public functions can make such a claim. However, the glory of the evening is Entertainment.

Northumberland has a great musical tradition. There was not much else to do during the long winter evenings in the isolated hill steadings. From the hills long ago came a steady stream of fiddlers, pipers, singers and poets and they are coming still. Traditional music is very much a living thing in the Borders and new generations are picking up their fiddles or working the bellows of the mellow little Northumbrian pipes and writing their own tunes to play on them. Some of the men who play at the suppers are professional musicians who travel the world on the traditional music circuit. Others will be back shepherding or driving a tractor in the morning. Whichever, they will be listened to with rapt attention by the audience who knows that they are being presented with the best available. They know that for the six or seven quid cost of their ticket (including supper) they are getting performances that audiences around the world would pay much fine gold to hear.

Story-tellers are also part of the tradition; humorous story-telling is a fine art and we get some of the finest practitioners at the suppers. I would be deceiving you if I said that the content of most of the stories is particularly genteel. The story-tellers target their audience and the stories reflect the interests of most of those present, dealing with matters sexual, agricultural and sporting.

Let us consider the Poets: for yes, we have poetry readings as well. These are home-bred, vernacular poems and they tend to centre on matters that the audience can relate to: matters such as sex, farming and sport. Inevitable? Yes, of course, but why not?

So the evening progresses. The smooth running is enforced by the Chairman, the thunder of whose huge fist on the table is sufficient to guarantee the order.

On occasion, I have been called upon to speak at one or other of the suppers. No speaker can complain at being asked to face a Shepherds' Supper unprimed. The normal thing is for a speaker to have a bottle of whisky plonked on the table in front of him at the beginning of the evening. He is told that when he has finished that one, another will be instantly forthcoming.

Nor should you think that the end of the formal proceedings marks the end of the evening. The music and the singing and the sipping is likely to continue until such times as it is thought that the licensing authorities might have cause to raise an eyebrow. It is not unknown for the survivors to adjourn to private property where there is likely to be yet more singing and sipping and crack (crack in the rural sense, which means good and amusing conversation, not something you stick up your nose). It is not unusual for Shepherds' Supperers to go straight home and change into their working clothes to begin another day.

Shepherds' Suppers are meet, right and a duty that I am grateful to be bound to.

Point-to-points are things that the Backwoodsman may well turn his attention to in March. Indeed, the more lissom sort of Backwoodsman may well take part — but not this one, no fear.

My old father rode in a lot of point-to-points as a young man, but it has never greatly interested me. At the time when I might just have made the weight (12st 7lbs), I had neither the money nor the ability. Even if I were now able to afford the expense of a point-to-point horse, I still would not have the ability (or the bottle) and would not get within 8 stone of the weight, even with a racing saddle. So as I have little personal involvement with point-to-points, I take little interest in them.

But what is a point-to-point anyway? It used to be an end-of-hunting jolly, where you lined up with your hunters at Point A and galloped across country to Point B, where you finished — always provided that you were not upside down in a ditch on the way.

Things, times and the countryside changed. The course and the racing gradually became more formal and specialised and official. At last the whole thing came under the wing of the Jockey Club. The courses became like park courses and the whole thing is a coarse version of National Hunt racing, but there are certain differences. For instance: only "amateur" riders can take part in a point-to-point. Point-to-points (I am sorry but I refuse to endorse the modern usage of "Points"; it is like calling Nigel "Nige"; ugh!) can only be organised by hunts recognised by one of the Masters of Hounds Associations and all horses that run in point-to-points must have a Master's certificate to say that they have been "regularly and fairly hunted".

Oh dear, oh dear; what a wealth of trials and tribulations are contained in the words "regularly and fairly hunted". The trouble lies in the fact that most point-to-point horses are no longer hunters, they are race horses and expensive to boot. They are temperamentally unsuited to jumping a four-foot post-and-rails off their hocks. Should they land in that strand of wire on the far side, then there is an awful lot of expensive horse flesh being instantly shredded and devalued. For all these reasons, point-to-point enthusiasts are reluctant to commit their horses to the rough and tumble of the hunting field proper. Many content themselves with coming to the meet, raising their hat to the Master and titupping genteelly about the roads for a couple of hours.

Even appearing at the meet can be fraught with difficulty. Point-to-point horses tend to be highly bred and highly strung. The point-to-point horse that boots two hounds for six over the boundary of the pub car park and attempts to eat another is certainly going to catch the Master's attention. The Master is then likely to bring the full force of that attention to bear upon the horse's rider. The scene that follows may be a painful one.

It is my experience that any point-to-point horse is capable of kicking the eye out of a gnat. I certainly do not want the nasty things anywhere near my hounds. When presented with a "Hunter's Certificate" for signature, I used to have only one question: "has the bugger paid his subscription?"

As a young man, however, I used to attend point-to-points fairly regularly. I vividly remember my first point-to-point as an MFH. No, that is not entirely true, I do not remember too much about it. But I have heard the story often and watched its continuously embroidered progress over the years with a certain amount of interest.

Not to put too fine a point (ha! ha!) on it, I got very drunk. This will hardly surprise those who know me, but it did surprise the worthy ladies of the Hunt Committee. To them I was then still something of an unknown quantity with many surprises still in store. The worthy ladies were frankly horrified at this moral lapse by their young Master and were worried by its effect upon the farming community, many of whom were stalwart supporters of Bethesda and Ebenezer. As a damage limitation exercise, I was carried bodily from the tent, laid out in the back of the knacker truck, covered with the canvas sheet and thus driven home in odorous odium.

Since that memorable day, it has been down hill all the way with me and point-to-points. I am not interested in the horses, or the betting, although I did once have a coup.

I went to a point-to-point with a chap called Paddy and this was the only reason for backing a 20–1 no-hoper called Paddy's Profit. It won in a canter because every other horse in the race fell. It was a memorable day indeed which finished up with an even more memorable evening in the Sergeant's Mess at Pirbright — but that is another story and outside the Backwoodsmanly scope.

Nowadays I only attend point-to-points under extreme pressure, even unto and including my own hunt's point-to-point.

Just occasionally Sir Ranulph summons me to his presence and gives me a stern homily on my duties as a Master of Hounds. This will often happen when the point-to-point is looming on the horizon. He then says that it is with great regret that he has discovered that certain pressures of business make it imperative that he should be in Greece, or Bermuda, or Bangkok or some other such grisly place beyond the pale of civilisation, just when he should be enjoying himself at our point-to-point. It is therefore, he says (bringing the whole force of his considerable personality into play) imperative, *absolutely imperative* that I form up and attend the point-to-point and man the Sponsors' Tent. Each year I swear it will be my last as dutyman; the next year always sees me thus commanded.

This sponsor business is all part of Nouveau Point-au-Point. What happens is that the hunt persuades groups of local businessmen to put up the prize money for the different races. In return for this, details of their philanthropy and their business are blazoned all over the race card:

"Adjacent Hunts Maiden Race sponsored by Bloggs Pre-Stressed Tubing Ltd" and hurrah for Mr Bloggs and the Maidens say I. In addition to this blaze of advertising, the sponsors get entertained. Allow me to set the scene for you just a little.

Our point-to-point takes place on a windswept steppe that overlooks the grey crawl of the North Sea. The next bit of high ground to the east is the Ural Mountains.

The special point-to-point wind gets brewed up in that mountainous range, and it sets off across the Russian Steppes, winding up as it goes. It pauses briefly over the Prussian plain to pick up a little Teutonic brutality; it hones its edge over the sea and lands with a vicious scream on our point-to-point course.

Somewhere here, amongst the announcer's caravan, marquees, and ladies' lavatories, there is erected a small grey tent, through whose loosely-laced interstices the wind howls with barely checked force. Over the entrance there is a rudely painted sign saying "Sponsors". Within the tent there will be found a huge stack of crates of whisky and a shivering wizened figure, the chattering of whose teeth may be heard even above the wolf wail of the wind: this is the Master in Charge of Entertaining Sponsors.

It has to be said that the word "sponsor" gets pretty loosely interpreted by the point-to-pointing public. The most unlikely people insinuate themselves through the tent flap and stand there rubbing their hands and smiling ingratiatingly. As I do not have a clue what any of the sponsors look like and as I will have already taken some fairly firm cold prevention treatment, I tend to hand out the hooch on a fairly liberal basis. And if a friend should stick his head through the entrance, then it seems only right to bring him inside for a stiffener and to share in my pleasure in listening to Mr Bloggs discoursing on the problems facing the Pre-Stressed Tube industry: it is riveting stuff and gets even better after the first half hour. By the end of the day (by which time Mr Bloggs will be well into the fascinating topic of the Hydraulic Galvanising Technique) the tent tends to bulge and steam a bit. By this time, also, I am thoroughly weatherproofed and dispensing alcoholic largesse in a grand and expansive manner. There is a longer queue outside my tent than there is outside the ladies' loo. The Point-to-Point Secretary is raising his horrified eyes unto the heavens and even the Constabulary start nipping in through the back flap when they think that the sergeant might not be looking. I did say what jolly fun point-to-pointing ish, didn't I? Hee! hee! hee!

The last time that I was left in charge of the sponsors' tent, it was calculated that it consumed the entire profit from the point-to-point. The pressure that used to be put on me to attend has slackened noticeably.

Another major event in March is the Hunter Trials.

A hunter trial is yet another form of equine competition. The competitors (sometimes with riders more or less attached) go round a course of specially built fences. If the riders fall off, or their steeds refuse at a fence, they get penalty points and they are timed either over all, or a section of, the course.

It has always been my firm contention that a horse has only two functions in this world: it should be either following hounds or contributing to their well being as Plat du Jour: behind hounds, or inside them, in other words. I regard all horse-related sports as skull-numbingly boring — although not as boring as things like football and tennis which are really the pits. However those are not sports anyway and therefore do not concern Backwoodsmen. Hunter trials do.

It has become an established tradition that I act as Starter at our hunter trials. There are two reasons for this.

The first is that I have a very loud voice. With throat of brass, lungs of leather, and vocal cords made muscular by years of making myself heard above the excesses of the English weather, I am a walking Public Address System.

The second reason is that, like any Master of Hounds who has survived the course as long as I have, I have developed a certain force of personality which I can bring to bear in moments of stress; or, if you wish the thing put more demotically, I do not take nonsense from anybody. This can be quite important. Hunter trial people can be very competitive, and the competitive urge combined with very proper nerves, from being more or less loosely attached to half a ton of highly strung horse flesh, does not always bring out the best in people. Under these circumstances, people can lose something of their normal charm of manner and attempt to impose their will upon officials charged with the smooth running of the proceedings. Not with me they do not. At least, they do not try it more than once.

Brian, Artie and I man the start.

The first thing that we do is to form our vehicles into a protective laager around which the mounted contestants prowl like Comanches itching for their Scalp of the Day.

The next thing we do is to break out the self-loading glasses. The day will be long and a heavy calibre drink should be ready to hand at all times.

We have CB radio contact with the fence builders, the judge, the secretary and very likely NATO HQ for all I know.

What happens is that competitors come and put down their numbers which we chalk on a blackboard and that is the order of starting: "first come, first served"; all very simple. All very simple except that having put down their number and impressed upon you that it is a matter of life and death and honour that they should start as soon as possible, they then swan off to do whatever it is that ladies do when they are about to start anything (the competitors tend to be 90 percent female) and disappear off the face of the earth.

"Number 97," bellows the Collecting Ring Steward. "Number 97, you're next." There is no response. "NUMBER 97, ARE YOU READY?" And answer comes there none. So you set away number 35 and then 48 and very likely number 3. Then number 97 will come trolling up saying surely it must be her turn by now, and poor, dear Sultan Raschid (her horse not her husband: he is called Mutley) is getting sooo cooold and figety. It will then be pointed out that she failed to make herself available when called and has missed her turn. The lady will immediately throw some species of wobbly. The way to deal with this is for me to turn up my megaphone to Maximum, the better to reason with her in a christian spirit.

In fact, my real job is much more demanding. The competitors are set off at two-minute intervals, so I stand festooned in stop watches shouting, "One minute . . . 30 seconds . . . 15 seconds . . . $10 - 9 - 8 - 7 - 6 - 5 - 4 - 3 - 2 - 1 - $ GO!" You have got to admit that it is a pretty snappy bit of patter, but after some eight hours, I have to admit that it can just begin to pall on you somewhat.

One becomes grateful for a bit of gossip in between, as it were. The trouble is that a good bit of gossip can be very distracting. You just get to the good bit and are exclaiming: "You don't mean it? . . . handcuffs *and* a dog collar . . . cramp, you say? . . . what, both together on the stretcher . . . ?" when there is an explosion on the CB as might be indicative of a judge who feels that he is being victimised by those in whom he has mistakenly reposed his trust. You have missed a two-minute slot. You will have to boldly look in the eye the competitor who has already been waiting rigid with nerves for three minutes too long and say: "One minute . . ."

Hunting in March is getting pretty fag endy in most countries. I am usually more than ready to finish by the end of March. The foxes disappear for one thing, the vixens start lying to ground and I prefer to leave them so. Of course, we have a job to do as well and if there is trouble, or potential trouble, with hill lambing in sight, then we have to deal with it.

Scenting conditions can be very difficult in March and, all in all, it will have been a long season since we started early in August. Everybody is getting just a bit stale.

Mind you, if you do have a good hunt in March, it can be a stormer.

"I'm not coming out there to fool about in those woods," said Derek. "I'm going off to the Mugwumps; they're meeting at a good place." The occasion we were discussing was an invitation meet for my hounds in a neighbouring country.

The neighbouring Master and I had hatched this one late at night when we were both in a highly elevated frame of mind. The idea had not seemed quite so good to him the next morning. In fact, nothing seemed very good to him the next morning.

The idea was received with a marked lack of enthusiasm by my friend's Joint Masters who looked at it in much the same light as the Romans must have felt when told that the Visigoths were coming round for a bit of a jolly.

The original idea had been to take my hounds to one of the better bits of neighbouring country and there to frolick. The idea got further and further downgraded until the meet was finally fixed in a howling waste of woodland where nobody wanted to go much anyway.

It is often said that one of the great things about hunting is its glorious uncertainty: sometimes it plays a joker.

To begin with, it looked as though Derek had been right. The local foxes all did their best to emulate the

Oozlum bird who, it will be remembered, deceived its enemies by running in ever decreasing circles until it eventually disappeared up its own — yes, well.

Then we found a fox, a good fox, a travelling fox, a fox still rank with the excesses of the night, who set out for home. It was one of those days with a holding scent, when hounds never really went terribly fast, but never really checked very much and when they did, they would cast themselves at the gallop, hit off the line and away again, and again, and again.

Details of a hunt that you did not take part in and in a country you do not know can be somewhat tedious. Suffice it to say that after some time it became clear that the home the fox was heading for was back in our own country. It was, in fact, in the back of a small village, nine and a half miles in a straight line from where we found him, although it was many more miles as he had run.

This old fox must have indeed had strong priapic tendencies because the purlieus of the village positively exploded with his extended family and there were foxes going all ways.

Enough seemed to be enough. There were horses and people spread over half the county; the afternoon was dry and hot and the horses were down to a walk, so we picked up the hounds and went and sat in a friendly farm yard, whilst transport was arranged.

The Mugwumps did not have a good day. In fact they did not find a fox. Derek was not exactly gruntled as he drove home. The sight of his face when he turned into his yard and found us sitting there is a memory that I shall treasure always.

★   ★   ★

I suppose that someone is going to ask me about whether, or not, I go to Cheltenham and/or Aintree in March. In case some of you are wondering why anyone should wish to go to such unlikely places anyway, perhaps I should explain "Cheltenham" is Backwoods shorthand for the National Hunt Festival meeting which includes the Gold Cup; "Aintree" is shorthand for the Grand National.

It is certainly true that you may well see some prime examples of Backwoodsmen at both meetings; indeed, Cheltenham and Aintree may well be a very good chance to examine large gatherings of these shy, furry, little creatures whiffling their whiskers and communicating with each other in a strange patois that seems to consist mainly of grunts and high-pitched laughter. They will all be wearing their spring plumage of felt hats, covert coats, and huge binocular cases festooned in badges. But what, I hear you cry, shall the female of the species be wearing? How on earth should I know? What am I; a fashion correspondent yet?

At one time I used to attend the Gold Cup meeting and quite enjoyed it. In fact I had my one big punt there, just after I left school. I started with a ten bob bet (representing 50 percent of my available capital) and went right through the card, plonking all my accumulated winnings on the next race. Memory is a fickle thing, but I seem to remember the whole pot going on a horse called Ennis Boy in the last, who came home at 12–1. I can still remember the glorious feeling of stuffing that great wad of notes in my pocket. I had never seen so much money in my life.

Two positive things came out of that day.

The first was that I went to a tailor and had my first adult stable of good clothes built around me. The second thing was that whilst I grew out of the clothes, I never grew out of the realisation that I had had a once in a lifetime Coup, which I was never likely to repeat. I have never gambled seriously since.

As my old father always said: "Only bet with bookies' money."

To add weight to the moral content of this tale (and we must have a little moral content in this book), some years later I was shown round the estate of a retired bookmaker: magnificent house, stud, racing stables, farm, broad acres. It was properly known as the Hinton Mackerel Manor Estate. I have reason to believe that the owner always referred to his property as EMA: Every Mug Assisted. A tour of such a place should be compulsory on all young persons before they place their first bet.

Back to Cheltenham: or not in my case. The last time I went there was in 1972. I decided that it had become unacceptably crowded. You could only get a drink when racing was actually happening and you could only have watched the racing when everybody was in the bar between the races — if you see what I mean.

I know that we are enjoined to love our fellow man, but I find it hard to love him in Horde Form. By all means go to Cheltenham and Aintree. Let yourself be jostled, elbowed, kicked, stepped on by the forces of Corporate Entertainment. Just do not expect to see me there. I shall watch the National and the Gold Cup from the comfortable deeps of my armchair and I shall see more than any of you.

April

Let us wax poetic:

> "Oh, to be in England
> Now that April's there."

All jolly fine for that silly ass Browning (not a Backwoodsmanly poet) to go wittering on about "blossoms and dewdrops and buttercups" and things: the wretched chap was sitting in a villa in Italy tanking up on the vino with a lot of other long-haired layabouts. What did he know about April? He certainly did not know about April in the Cheviots. No, no, I think the true mood of the English spring is much better encapsulated in a Dartmoor rhyme written by my old friend Wilfred John Anonymous:

> "Vust er rained,
> then er blawed,
> then er 'ailed,
> then er snawed,
> then er comed a shooer of rain,
> then er vruz and blawed again."

(Pause for Parenthesis: you will notice that I have written er and not 'er. Most people would write "'er" and make some jocular and patronising allusion to the propensity of "simple country folk" to make all objects female, as when you look at the tractor and say, "Reckon er's brokken, you." *Er* has nothing to with *her*: *er* is Saxon for *it*. You simple town chappies could not be expected to know that, you poor hignorant things.)

Any road up, Old Wilfred John knew much more about the fickle nature of the English Spring than silly Browning would, fanning himself on his melon patch.

For the Backwoodsman, April means Lambing and Lambing means Lambing Storms. The Lambing Storm is one of nature's sneakier and nastier manifestations. I remember one in particular. It came on a Friday night and for twenty-four hours this black wind screamed out of the north, driving horizontal snow and sleet with it. It was the middle of April and came suddenly after a fine settled spell. We had been trolling around in our shirt sleeves telling each other what grand lambing weather it was, then Whammo.

I was lucky; I had only just started lambing and I could keep everything contained in my shed whilst the storm screamed and slavered outside. Not everybody was fortunate enough to have that option and little lambs out in the open had no chance in that ferocious weather. I know one man who picked up fifty pathetic little corpses on one morning. That is the sort of thing that makes a strong man weep.

Let us not get into the trauma of lambing just yet though. I think that we should have a little break before all that hard work.

In April sensible Backwoodsmen go staghunting, although it is some years since I have been able to get to Exmoor and this is a source of great regret to me.

I do not think that this is the place to argue the rights and wrongs of the hunting of red deer. Backwoodsmen have no doubts but that it is meet and right and that the end of staghunting would mean the end of red deer on Exmoor. In April the young stags are hunted and this is when the long straight hunts tend to happen. Back-woodsmen from all over England come to Exmoor for the Spring Staghunting.

Exmoor has always held a special place in my affections. It used to be satisfyingly wild and woolly, rather like Northumberland in fact. It may be that its special spirit will be threatened by the increasing improvement of communications. As an old friend of mine said when we were gloomily watching the march of the M4 motorway westwards, slicing off the very south-western tip of the Cotswolds.

"Tidn't the drain I mind so much; it's the effluence that's going to come flowing down it that worries me" — except he didn't use the word "effluence" because he didn't know how to spell it. The southern parts of Gloucestershire are now an outer suburb of London and full of perfectly frightful people who are exterminating all the Backwoodsmen.

The same thing has happened to my dear old Dartmoor and I expect that the poison cloud of yuppification is poised over Exmoor, if it has not already landed.

Anyway this is a tale of long ago and feckless youth and the Old Exmoor.

"Let us go staghunting," said Auntie Vi. "The horses are still fit and Cedric will drive us all up in that huge vehicular brothel he calls a horse box." I thought that this was an absolutely spiffing idea. I had just finish a long, hard season hunting hounds and was ready for a bit of a jolly.

It meant an early start. It was a long haul through the twisting Devon roads, but we were all immensely comfortable in the Vehicular Brothel: a truly sumptuous machine.

A brief dissertation on the technique of staghunting. The stag to be hunted is selected by the Harbourers. They are local men with immense and intimate knowledge of red deer. They will have been out the previous day watching the grazing herds; they will select a stag of the right age and condition and will then watch to see where he lies up. The skill is to get the chosen stag separated from the rest of the herd and running. This is done by the

Tufters. The Tufters are a few selected old hounds. They are taken to the covert and their job is to hunt the selected stag out into the open. This is a very bald summary of a highly skilled proceeding. It may take twenty minutes, or it may take four hours. Once the stag is away, the Tufters are stopped and the rest of the pack, who have been shut up in some convenient farm, are brought up and laid on, then the hunt proper begins.

I only had one horse that day and if you only have one horse it is best to save him and watch and listen from the top of the combe. The hunt staff with the staghounds will ride two, or even three horses, during the day. So you stand with your reins looped over your arm and smoke and chat and listen.

Shrill whistle blasts and a man galloping up. Instant action. Everybody is frantically checking their girths. The whipper-in who has been leaning nonchalantly against the barn wall opens the door, releases a frantic tide of excited hounds and vaults into his saddle. We are off.

The young stag, once separated from his companions, tends to run fairly straight. This one set off right out over the Forest — Forest as in old Royal Hunting Ground and nothing to do with sitka spruce. The high wide top of Exmoor is the Forest.

Go right over the top of Exmoor and you are likely to cross the Chains. This is the central sponge where all the local rivers rise. It is a bit wet or, as they say in Devon, "stuggy".

The splendid folk of Exmoor get very exercised about the wet ground, whilst the Dartmoor folk tend to be rather patronising and say that they do not know what the "stuggy" really is. The old saying is that on Exmoor you can ride anywhere except where you can't and on Dartmoor you can't ride anywhere except where you can. The thing being that Dartmoor is much wetter.

I was riding Red Knight who was one of the five best horses that I have ever owned. He cost me £150. A better Moor horse never looked through a bridle.

There is an art to riding the stuggy. A horse that starts to plunge will sink with all hands; the clever horse takes little tiny steps and skitters across the heaving peat and moss. I well remember, that day, people rolling and wallowing to right and left, with much wailing and regrettable language. Dear old Red Knight just skimmed across like one of those water boatmen insects. On and on we galloped, right over the top of the moor and down towards the sea.

There were very few people left when the stag was eventually taken. "Taken" means that the stag stands at bay and is dispatched with a humane killer. It had been an eleven-mile point and this meant that everybody was many miles from their transport.

The staghunters are well used to this situation. The select few who had got to the end took their horses to the farm belonging to the Joint Master, which was handy by. Some held the horses, the others piled into Land Rovers and went off in search of their boxes.

Cedric had fallen by the wayside so Auntie Vi left me with her horse and Red Knight, and some firm instructions. I regret to say that Auntie Vi had little faith in the moral strength of my character. I still carry in my head the picture of a packed Land Rover driving away full of people and the mortal remains of the stag on which Auntie Vi was somewhat precariously perched.

I was obviously in for a long wait and so I sat on a bank in the sun whilst the two tired horses picked a bit of grass.

"'Scuse me, sir, but Mr Nancekivell say will 'ee step into the house. I'll take the 'osses."

Bob Nancekivell was then Master of the staghounds: a huge, lovely man, a big man in every way.

"Come in, come in; you'm welcome. You'll have a drink?" Well, you know me. It was a happy party. It was deemed to be one of the best hunts for many years.

"You've brought us luck," they cried. "My Dear Life, your glass is empty." It was never empty for long. For two happy hours we laughed and roistered and sang. The whisky was coming in half pint glasses and I kicked my little legs in the air and laughed and laughed . . .

"There's a box come to pick 'ee up. They'll tak 'ee to Simonsbath. Your folk will meet 'ee there," they said at last. I rose to my feet with great solemnity, shook hands all round, embraced my hostess, walked through the door into the fresh air and gently folded up into a heap on the ground.

To put in perspective what happened next, you must remember (a) that I was very young, indeed the youngest MFH in the country at that time and (b) that I had eaten nothing since a hasty egg of 0555 hours.

"I'm not 'aving 'ee in my box," said the driver. "Zuppose he'm sick all over the cab?"

"'Tidn't no trouble. Tell 'ee what us'll do. Now lift 'un. Steady now. Bugger 'eem some weight, mind. Now get 'un in the seat. Hold 'un up straight. Now shut the door. Now put 'is 'ead out the window. That's it, now wind the window up so 'ee can't get 'is 'ead back in. There now, that's a Proper Job: don't matter if 'ee is zick now."

In this way I travelled from Oare to Simonsbath.

At Simonsbath, the Vehicular Brothel waited with a disapproving Cedric and a hand-wringing Auntie Vi, for news had flown before as ill tidings always do.

"'Yere 'ee is then," they cried, opening the door so that I cascaded out.

Thus I ended my first day's staghunting, flat on my back in the middle of the road at Simonsbath, making a valiant effort to sing the "Wearing of the Green".

I have a slot of the stag on my desk as I write and every time I have been to Exmoor since, someone has always sidled up to me and said: "Do 'ee mind the time us 'ad that good hunt and took the stag below Mr Nancekivell's place and then you . . ."

Oh yes, I mind the time all right; that day is etched in gold in my memory.

We finish our own hunting at the beginning of April. Over the previous month we have been retreating further and further back into the hills as the in-bye (low ground) lambing gathers momentum. As we shall see, lambing is a time of maximum effort and raw nerve ends; even the keenest hunting farmer does not want the added distraction of a pack of hounds through his lambing field.

We still have a job to do out-bye. The hill flocks do not start lambing until the third week in April and, not to put too fine a point on it, they do not want too many foxes about when they do start. Yes, I know that there are people who discount the possibility of foxes feasting on lamb and who stoutly maintain that foxes exist solely on a diet of nut cutlets and yoghurt. The fact is that hill foxes will take hill lambs. They are especially inclined to take the first born of a pair of twins whilst the ewe is groaning and straining with number two. Not every fox will take lambs, but once one gets a taste for lamb, it will kill for the sake of killing. The hill shepherds want to reduce the chances of this happening by having the fox population at an acceptable level by the start of lambing.

Thus it is that we spend the last few days' hunting in the wilder and more inaccessible parts of the hills and some long hard days we have of it too.

Mind you there are some lovely days at that time of year. Take the other day, for instance.

Rupert and I had bumped and chugged our way to the very top of one of the very highest hills. There was a warm spring sun and a cool spring breeze. The curlews were whistling, the whimbrels were, well, whimbrelling and, far below me, in the wooded valleys, hounds were running hard in several lots on several different foxes.

I ought to have gone down and taken a closer interest, but I felt positively surplus to requirements and end of seasonish. There were plenty of people farting about down there; they did not need me. So I took my bait bag and the binoculars and found a nice little fold in the ground that just nicely fitted my back and there I settled down to watch and listen.

Jock tells me that in certain clear weather conditions you can see the hills of the Lake District from the top of that hill. Even the most optimistic crow would make that a distance of eighty miles. You could not see quite that far on that day, but you could still see fold upon fold of hills marching away in the blue distance to what must have been the northern end of the Pennines.

Far below me I could hear one lot of hounds coming

closer. There were not many of them from the cry. I turned my glasses onto the edge of the trees and there was a flash of movement: a fox, yes, yes indeed.

I never fail to be excited by the sight of a fox.

With unhurried stride he slipped across the open and disappeared into the broken ground of the peat hags at the burn head.

A few minutes later hounds came into sight: only two and a half couple and no one with them. They paused on the edge of the trees and then hit off the line of my fox and sang away across the heather.

There were more hounds running down on my right. This sounded like a bigger lot. I swung the glasses round, but they were running just inside the trees and, although I could hear them well, I could not see them. Yet more hounds were running far down the valley below the old ruined steading.

There was only one thing for it.

I got out the sandwiches and the thermos and poured myself a cup of tea.

I have to admit that I am getting pretty stale by the time April comes in. It is a long time since we started at the beginning of August and hounds, horses and men are all showing signs of wear and tear. Also lambing looms ever nearer and occupies more and more of my thoughts. The one thing that I am quite certain about is that lambing and hunting do not mix.

There was a dreadful year when I got it wrong.

You see, I normally try to time things so that there is at least a week between the end of hunting and the start of lambing.

Sometimes it works.

Sometimes the timing comes badly unstuck.

One year I was going round the sheep about ten days before the end of hunting. This was in the old pre-shed days and the ewes were out on a bit of rough pasture. I noticed a ewe out on her own and as I got nearer I saw two little prick ears sticking up from the behind a bull snout (grass tussock). It was a new born lamb.

"Go back from whence you came!" I cried. "You should not be here until the seventh of April."

"Maaa!" said the lamb and ma promptly popped out another one.

I will not harrow you with the account of the days (and nights) that followed. It is sufficient to say that I have proved conclusively that it is not good to hunt hounds all day and lamb all night. I well remember going to sleep in the saddle on the last day of the season.

The last day of the season is always a mixture of relief and tristesse. The end of another season that we shall not see again.

We are all another year older even if we are not much wiser or richer. Indeed, we should probably all be much wiser and richer if we gave up hunting altogether, but I do not think that we should be much happier.

I might think of all these things as Rupert and I trundle homewards from the last meet.

I might think of the moment when I first became a Master and Huntsman in 1964. I might think of all the planning and striving and scheming that led up to that great (and I have to say unlikely) moment. I might cast my mind back over all the years that followed: the triumphs, the disasters; the many kind people and the few (very few) bloody ones; the sights, the sounds, the feel of a good horse between the knees, that I shall never know again.

Most of all, I might think about the hounds. It was love of the foxhound that led me into my somewhat eccentric way of life. It was love of the foxhound that drove me on through all the years until that April day in 1985 when I put my horn back into the case on the saddle and said goodbye to my hounds on the last occasion when they would be really mine. I am not going to bore you by telling you what I truly felt at that moment; let us just say that I knew that my life was never going to be quite the same again.

All this and more I might reflect upon and if I get a little maudlin, well, that is no one's worry but mine. Anyway, there is not too much time for introspection: it is time for me to become a busy flockmaster and for Rupert to put on his tractoring hat: the Lambing is upon us.

The Lambing is the culmination of the shepherd's year: it is his harvest.

An old man once said to me: "If you don't enjoy lambing, you shouldn't keep sheep." I do enjoy lambing, when I am not hating it. Lambing is a time of raw emotions, bloodshot eyes, unshaven chins and a deep, deep weariness.

At lambing time I work a twenty-hour day. I snatch sleep in dribs and drabs when I can. I become a walking, breathing, temper looking for somewhere to explode. And yet, and yet there is an adrenalin factor and a satisfaction. I dread the coming of lambing and am mightily relieved when it is over, but I think that I would miss it; I really think I would.

It is the nights that get to me.

I always do the nights; help cometh in the morning, usually about 0800, but the nights are mine alone. The secret of successful lambing is constant vigilance. We offer our ladies a twenty-four-hour service.

For two dreary years I lived in a caravan during lambing, returning home only to eat and bathe, sitting through the long nights with book, thermos and bottle of whisky. My lot has now much improved. The shed with the ewes is just across the yard from the house. I can wander across the yard in my carpet slippers if the weather is dry and return to the comfort of my own armchair and fireside, but the nights are still a dreary time. I would much prefer to be tucked up in bed.

My tried and trusted companion (and adversary) through many lambing nights is my old tin alarm clock. *"CLAAAAANNNNGGGG!"* I wake up with a jolt and the book falls off my lap to the floor as I fumble for the stop button. I hate the alarm clock.

It is one o'clock in the morning and time for a round of the shed. The house is silent except for the ticking of the grandfather clock. I stumble out to the kitchen, rubbing my eyes; the dogs do not even bother to stir. I pull on my waders (handy for kneeling), huddle into my thick jacket and pull a woollen cap down over my ears. The torch, the torch; where did I put the torch?

I listen as I cross to the darkened shed. Silence is a relief. A distressed blaring will indicate some sort of problem.

"All right, girls, it's only me." I always say this before I switch the lights on. It is not good to startle heavily pregnant ladies. They are used to my voice.

The shed has two alleyways with pens on either side. I walk slowly down one of the alleys looking from side to side, shining my torch into dark corners. Most of the ewes are asleep, some of them are lying quietly chewing their cud and blinking in the light.

A thin wind rattles the roof of the shed and I burrow deeper into the jacket.

Through the open doors at the bottom of the shed, I can see the lights of a solitary car sweeping up the valley road; not many folk about at this time of night.

Although I want the lambing to get done, I always cherish a secret hope that nothing will be happening, then I can return to the armchair, stir up the fire, and snatch a little more treasured sleep.

Ah no; it is not to be. In the bottom pen on the west side, a solitary ewe is standing in a corner pawing at the straw. She is restless. As she turns, I can see the little transparent bladder protruding. She has "put her water out"; a lamb is on the way. It could be fifteen minutes; it could be two hours. Whatever, that has knackered the chance of sleep since she will have to be monitored.

Everything else seems quiet so I go back to the kitchen and make myself a cup of Bovril, my mainstay on the long night watch.

The mug drained, it is time to have another look.

Well here is a turn up. An unexpected pair of twins on the east side, shelled out like peas; that is the way to do it. The first arrival is already on its feet, shaking and wobbling as it tries to nuzzle its way to the tit for that first drink. The other has obviously just dropped and the good old ewe is licking it enthusiastically. No problem there except that another ewe who has not lambed is also licking it enthusiastically. Some ewes would claim every lamb in the shed if they were allowed to.

We cannot have that so I carry both lambs through the gate and put them in the passage followed by the anxious mother. The would-be mother would also like to join the party and gets a belt round the lug; patience is in short supply in the small hours.

The Lamb Pram is my own invention. It is a small cage on wheels. I pop the twins into it and set off up the passage towing it behind me. The ewe can see, hear and smell her children and follows willingly.

At the top of the shed there is a series of single pens where the recently lambed ewes are shut up with their offspring so that the vital mothering bond can be established without interference and in peace. First, each lamb has to have its antibiotic pill (pushed down the throat with a practised finger) and has to have the still raw navel sprayed with antibiotic spray to prevent infection getting in. A bucket of water and a fold of hay and that is them set for the moment.

Now what about that ewe that I came out to look at. She is down and straining, her top lip curling. Time for a quick check. A gentle probe with a finger and there is a little nose and two little front feet: a good presentation and all as it should be: let nature take its course for the time being.

Nature is making a poorish job of it further up the alley. Another ewe is straining and she is patently in trouble. It is a head first job; that is the lamb's head is through the pelvis but the front feet are back. It is intervention time.

Back to the house for a bucket of warm water. Then wash the hands and rub on some antiseptic lambing oils. The poor ewe is straining and paining. What I have got to do, kneeling in the straw, is to push the head right back inside, find the front feet, and get the three coming out together. Sounds easy, does it not?

As gently as possible I work the head back into the womb. I am in a warm, dark, wet world where I can see only with my finger tips. I close my eyes to concentrate all my senses there.

The ewe clamps her pelvis on my wrist. "Ouch! you hard bitch," but I do not blame her; I would not want me sticking my hand up me, if you see what I mean.

A foot, but which foot? I work my fingers up it and find a hock so it's a hind leg which is no good to me. And there is another head — twins. So not only have I got to find the front feet but I have got to find the correct front feet . . .

It takes half an hour, but at last we reach the triumphant moment when I ease the slimy bundle into the world and present it to its exhausted mother for its maternal licking.

I go to the medicine tray and draw off a hypodermic syringe of penicillin and a huge syringe of calcium to combat the effect of stress. Blow me down, out pops the other lamb, no problem at all. I will leave her quiet with her lambs for the moment and have a look round.

In the other passage, there are two frantic ewes and four new-born lambs. One ewe has decided that all four must be hers and is warding off the other frantic parent: time for a touch of the Solomons.

By five o'clock the grey dawn is starting to seep over the hills. I take my current mug of Bovril and lean on the yard gate to watch the start of another day (or the finish of another night) and to listen to the curlews in the valley.

Then it is time to give the ewes their breakfast and to attend to some more births, until my nose starts to twitch: is it — ? Can it be — ? yes, there is no doubt; it is the magical smell of cooking bacon wafting across the yard and in my mind I see the eggs, the rolls, the monstrous pot of tea and then that supreme moment when I put my feet on the stool, pour another cup of tea and light that first (and most important) pipe of the day.

At that moment all the weariness and worry of the night falls away and is replaced with a quiet satisfaction.

At that moment I quite enjoy lambing and, after all, if you do not enjoy lambing you should not keep sheep.

By the end of April, the lambing will be finished, all except for the few inevitable tail-enders. There are few nicer things than leaning on your stick in the warm spring sunshine watching a field of contented ewes and well-fed lambs revelling in the sun and the fresh spring grass.

It might even make a Backwoodsman think about his world and his life.

I wonder how much future there is for him? Can there be a place for Backwoodsmen in the Brave New Britain? I am not very sanguine for him. The Backwoodsman represents a way of life that is fast disappearing. He and that way of life have survived precisely because he was happy to live and have his being in the wilder and remoter places: in the Backwoods, where nobody else wanted much to be. The rest of the population fled to the towns seeking Sophistication, Glamour, Excitement and I do not know what all.

In the search for these elusive commodities, Urban Man created conditions for himself which are quite rightly regarded as unacceptable for the animals themselves. As a result, he is now suffering from all those problems associated with animals kept in unnatural conditions: feather-pecking, tail-biting, hyper-tension et al. He has tried to alleviate these problems by sticking things in his arm and sniffing things up his nose: they do not work.

It is at this point that Urban Man remembers his maternal grandfather who farmed in Devon (every Urban Man has a grandfather who farmed in Devon). The memory of the maternal grandfather and his boorish Backwoods ways have always been an acute embarrassment to our Upwardly Mobile Urb. Then all of a sudden, Gaffer Brimicombe is Fashionable. He was not a drunken old sot who pursued milkmaids and foxes with equal vigour, he was "natural", "environment friendly", "organic"; or something. He may never have bathed, may have done his heavy thinking in an earth closet and removed a lot of knickers but he never made a hole in the ozone layer.

All of a sudden everybody wants the Backwoods. Everybody wants to re-establish their rural roots. But what of the Aboriginal Inhabitants?

The Backwoodsman who has been composting happily for generations suddenly finds his world turned upside down. His fields are full of brightly-coloured anoraks. His villages become full of Money Brokers or Well-Meaning Men in Beards and Sandals who want to be at one with Mother Earth (but they do not want pigs next door or mud in the lane).

His roads become straightened, widened, dual-laned and floodlit. He is to become homogenised, standardised, pasteurised, yuppified and very likely certified at the end of it all.

There will be no room in the New Britain for the Backwoodsman because there will be no Backwoods any more; his habitat will be destroyed.

The Backwoods are fast disappearing; if the politicians do not get them, then the developers will. In my opinion, the Backwoodsmen of England are in pretty much the same position as the Sioux Indians were when they topped that frightful fellow Custer: they are doomed and I do not suppose that there will be a British equivalent of the battle of Little Big Horn to mark their passing.

I suppose that some will survive. There will be Backwoods Theme Parks where token, and suitably tranquillised, Backwoodsmen will be on parade for the delectation of the New Plastic Britons. A few might be stuffed and displayed in museums. The remainder of the Backwoodsmen will just fade away in the woods, hills and marshes from whence they came.

I like to think that in the future, when all Britain is covered with motorways, megastores and executive housing, there will be somewhere a haunted shopping mall. A fat, red-faced, ghostly huntsman will thunder after his ghostly hounds down the central alley and they will catch their ghostly fox at the foot of the plastic palm tree outside the health food shop and the unisex hair salon. The ghastly phantasmagoria will then disappear leaving only a strong smell of whisky and Havana cigar.

In the meantime it is really too nice a day to worry over much. I am going down to the rough bank by the quarry and seek the crafty little corner which is sheltered from the wind and warmed by the sun and where the rock fits snugly into the back. In this way I shall finish this book in exactly the same place as I started it, which is a very Backwoodsmanly thing to do.

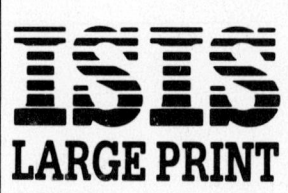

LARGE PRINT

If you have enjoyed reading this book, you will be pleased to know that many more titles are available.

We have listed a selection on the next few pages. These are printed in large print and some are also published by Isis in unabridged audio form. In addition, there are other titles, not listed here, which are only available from us as audio books.

Further information on these and many other titles, is available from the address below. Alternatively, contact your local library for details of what they have.

Any suggestions you may have for new large print or audio titles, would be very welcome.

**ISIS
55 St Thomas' Street
Oxford OX1 1JG
(0865) 250333**

General Non-Fiction

Michael Bright	**The Living World**
Estelle Catlett	**Track Down Your Ancestors**
Bruce Chatwin	**What Am I Doing Here**
Phil Drabble	**One Man and His Dog**
Jonathan Goodman	**The Lady Killers**
Anita Guyton	**Healthy Houseplants A-Z**
Duff Hart-Davis	**Country Matters**
William R Hartson	**Teach Yourself Chess**
Stephen W Hawking	**A Brief History of Time**
Dr Richard Lacey	**Safe Shopping, Safe Cooking, Safe Eating**
Doris Lessing	**Particularly Cats and More Cats**
Vera Lynn	**We'll Meet Again**
Desmond Morris	**The Animals Roadshow**
Desmond Morris	**Dogwatching**
Desmond Morris	**Catlore**
Frank Muir & Denis Norden	**You Have My Word**
Shiva Naipaul	**An Unfinished Journey**
John Pilger	**A Secret Country**
R W F Poole	**A Backwoodsman's Year**
Valerie Porter	**Faithful Companions**
Beryl Reid	**Beryl, Food and Friends**
Sonia Roberts	**The Right Way to Keep Pet Birds**
Yvonne Roberts	**Animal Heroes**
June Whitfield	**Dogs' Tales**
Ian Wilson	**Undiscovered**
Andrew Young	**A Prospect of Flowers**

Humour

Douglas Adams	**The Hitch Hiker's Guide to the Galaxy**
Mary Dunn	**Lady Addle Remembers**
	Echoes of Laughter
Giovanni Guareschi	**Don Camillo and the Devil**
Barry Pain	**The Eliza Stories**
Walter Carruthers Sellar & Robert Julian Yeatman	**1066 And All That**
Tom Sharpe	**Blott on the Landscape**
Tom Sharpe	**Porterhouse Blue**
Tom Sharpe	**Vintage Stuff** (A)
Tom Sharpe	**Wilt on High**
E OE Somerville & Martin Ross	**In Mr Knox's Country**
Sue Townsend	**True Confessions of Adrian Albert Mole, Margaret Hilda Roberts and Susan Lilian Townsend**

(A) Large Print books available in Audio

BIOGRAPHY AND AUTOBIOGRAPHY

Lord Abercromby	**Childhood Memories**
Margery Allingham	**The Oaken Heart**
Hilary Bailey	**Vera Brittain**
Trevor Barnes	**Terry Waite**
Winifred Beechey	**The Rich Mrs Robinson**
Sidney Biddle Barrows	**Mayflower Madam**
Christabel Bielenberg	**The Past Is Myself**
Ian Botham	**It Sort of Clicks**
Michael Burn	**Mary and Richard**
Winston S Churchill	**Memories and Adventures**
Denis Constanduros	**My Grandfather**
George Courtauld	**Odd Noises From the Barn**
Mary Craig	**The Crystal Spirit**
Peter Evans	**Ari**
Diana Farr	**Five at 10**
Joyce Fussey	**Calf Love**

BIOGRAPHY AND AUTOBIOGRAPHY

Joyce Fussey	**Cats in the Coffee**
Joyce Fussey	**Cows in the Corn**
Jon & Rumer Godden	**Two Under the Indian Sun**
William Golding	**The Hot Gates**
Michael Green	**The Boy Who Shot Down an Airship**
Michael Green	**Nobody Hurt in Small Earthquake**
Unity Hall	**Philip**
Unity Hall & Ingrid Seward	**Royalty Revealed**
Penny Junor	**Charles**
Imran Khan	**All Round View**
Julia Keay	**The Spy Who Never Was**
Margaret Lane	**The Tale of Beatrix Potter**
T E Lawrence	**Revolt in the Desert**
Bernard Levin	**The Way We Live Now**
Suzanne Lowry	**Cult of Diana**
Vincent V Loomis with Jeffrey L Ethell	**Amelia Earhart**

BIOGRAPHY AND AUTOBIOGRAPHY

Eugene McCarthy	**Up 'Til Now**
Jeanine McMullen	**Wind in the Ash Tree**
Peter Medawar	**Memoir of a Thinking Radish**
Spike Milligan	**Adolf Hitler: My Part in his Downfall** (A)
Jessica Mitford	**Hons and Rebels**
Eric Newby	**Something Wholesale**
Christopher Nolan	**Under the Eye of the Clock** (A)
Gerald Priestland	**The Unquiet Suitcase**
Siegfried Sassoon	**Memoirs of an Infantry Officer**
Ingrid Seward	**Diana**
Dolly Shepherd	**When the 'Chute Went Up**
Isaac Bashevis Singer	**Love and Exile**
Norman Tebbit	**Upwardly Mobile**
Andrew Thomson	**Margaret Thatcher**
Robert Westall	**The Children of the Blitz**
Ben Wicks	**The Day They Took The Children**

Fiction

Joan Aiken	**Blackground** (A)
Kingsley Amis	**One Fat Englishman**
Julian Barnes	**A History of The World in 10 1/2 Chapters** (A)
Stan Barstow	**Joby**
Samuel Beckett	**More Pricks Than Kicks**
Heinrich Böll	**The Lost Honour of Katharina Blum**
Jorge Louis Borges	**The Book of Sand**
Vera Brittain	**Account Rendered**
Vera Brittain	**Born 1925**
Anita Brookner	**A Start in Life**
Anthony Burgess	**The Piano Players** (A)
Truman Capote	**Breakfast at Tiffany's**
Peter Carey	**Oscar and Lucinda** (A)
J L Carr	**A Month in the Country**
Bruce Chatwin	**Utz**
Susan Cheever	**Doctors and Women**
Tessa Dahl	**Working for Love**
Margaret Drabble	**The Millstone**
William Faulkner	**The Sound and the Fury**
Penelope Fitzgerald	**The Beginning of Spring**
Jock Gallagher	**To the Victor the Spoils**
Jane Gardam	**The Sidmouth Letters**
David Garnett	**Aspects of Love**
André Gide	**La Symphonie Pastorale**
Stella Gibbons	**Cold Comfort Farm**
B M Gill	**Time and Time Again**

(A) Large Print books available in Audio

Fiction

Nadine Gordimer	**A Sport of Nature**
George & Weedon Grossmith	**The Diary of a Nobody**
Doris Grumbach	**The Magician's Girl**
O Henry	**Gift of the Magi**
Christopher Isherwood	**Goodbye to Berlin**
Thomas Keneally	**Towards Asmara**
Margaret Kennedy	**The Constant Nymph**
Rudyard Kipling	**The Light That Failed**
Gaston Leroux	**The Phantom of the Opera**
Doris Lessing	**The Grass is Singing**
Doris Lessing	**The Fifth Child (A)**
Eric Linklater	**Sealskin Trousers**
Penelope Lively	**Passing On (A)**
David Lodge	**Nice Work (A)**
Jack London	**The Call of the Wild**
Carson McCullers	**The Heart is a Lonely Hunter**
Bernard Malamud	**The Fixer**
David Malouf	**Harland's Half Acre**
Robin Maugham	**The Servant**
Brian Moore	**The Lonely Passion of Judith Hearne**
W Somerset Maugham	**The Moon & Sixpence**
Katharine Moore	**Moving House**
Iris Murdoch	**Under the Net**
Edna O'Brien	**Girls in Their Married Bliss**
Edna O'Brien	**A Pagan Place**
Boris Pasternak	**The Last Summer**
Alan Paton	**Cry, The Beloved Country**

(A) Large Print books available in Audio

Fiction

Anthony Powell	**The Fisher King**
J B Priestley	**The Shapes of Sleep**
Mary Renault	**The Bull From the Sea**
Mary Shelley	**Frankenstein**
Alan Sillitoe	**Out of the Whirlpool**
Elizabeth Smart	**By Grand Central Station I Sat Down and Wept**
John Steinbeck	**Cannery Row** (A)
Jan Struther	**Mrs Miniver**
Sir Rabindranath Tagore	**Crescent Moon**
Angela Thirkell	**Wild Strawberries**
Colin Thubron	**Falling**
Alice Walker	**Meridian**
Marina Warner	**The Lost Father**
Evelyn Waugh	**Men at Arms**
Evelyn Waugh	**A Handful of Dust**
Fay Weldon	**The Wife's Revenge**
Rebecca West	**Sunflower**
Tennessee Williams	**The Roman Spring of Mrs Stone**
Edmund Wilson	**Memoirs of Hecate County**
Virginia Woolf	**Flush**

(A) Large Print books available in Audio